"Magnificent. Absolutely magnificent. A grand slam through and through. A really fresh, meaningful and Ruthian addition to the history of Ruth."

— Baseball historian Tim Reid

"Wow what a wonderful book! Exciting and informative. *Babe Ruth — A Superstar's Legacy* has things I heard about the Babe from people who knew him well and lots more. A beautiful piece of writing!"   — Ray Negron, best-selling author, New York Yankees executive, and ESPN radio host

"There are many books about the legendary Babe Ruth, but Jerry Amernic takes the reader on a new path dedicated to the sheer impact of this man behind the classic rags-to-riches tale. *Babe Ruth — A Superstar's Legacy* goes beyond statistics and his storied career. It shows what an influential force he was, and still is, on our culture and the world. Amernic explains how a larger-than-life figure became the standard of dominance all others are measured against."

— Joe Orlando, CEO, Collectors Universe

"This is the first book to explore how the Babe Ruth League got off the ground and got to where it is today with over one million players playing under the name Babe Ruth. Jerry Amernic has written an intriguing book about the most recognized figure in baseball and a true American icon."

— Steve Tellefsen, President/CEO, Babe Ruth League, Inc.

"Jerry Amernic brilliantly tells the story of Babe Ruth as he is remembered today in so many ways – from contemporary youth baseball and merchandise branding to collectors' items and innumerable geographic locales. The book's subtitle is 'A Superstar's Legacy' but it's really about Babe Ruth The Superstar whose pre-eminence enthralls us to this day."   — Baseball historian William Humber

"*Babe Ruth — A Superstar's Legacy* sheds new light on Ruth as a man who was ahead of his time and not only on the baseball field, but also where he stood on racial segregation. There are many books about Babe Ruth, but this is the first one that really gets into the race issue. It's a masterpiece on the Babe!"

— Bill Jenkinson, author of *The Year Babe Ruth Hit 104 Home Runs* and *Babe Ruth: Against All Odds, World's Mightiest Slugger*

"*Babe Ruth — A Superstar's Legacy* gives readers an in-depth look at the person who defined baseball and still stands as the greatest player of all-time. Jerry Amernic chronicles the life of Ruth and the legacy he had on the sport, on America, and around the globe. This book has stories, insights, historical photographs, statistics and recollections of Ruth. A must read! You won't want to put it down."   — Bradford H. Turnow, New York Yankees baseball historian

"Considering baseball's enduring popularity, *Gift of the Bambino* has the makings of a family-oriented Hollywood movie, a cross between *The Natural* and *Field of Dreams*. It will make the perfect gift for a young baseball fan."
— *The Wall Street Journal*

"*Gift of the Bambino* is a love story that is peripherally about baseball. Babe Ruth's first home-run ball is the axis on which this tale of triumph and adversity turns. It is at times both heart-wrenching and heart-warming, and a thoroughly enjoyable read."
— W. P. Kinsella, author of *Shoeless Joe*
which was made into the film *Field of Dreams*

"Amernic makes a good case for baseball magic. This nostalgic look at the golden days of baseball is worth picking up."
— *The Oakland Tribune*

"This tale inevitably spurs the word 'heartwarming'. Amernic generates a sepia-tinted *Field of Dreams* nostalgia. The truly moving scenes show the loving counsel of old age, the awakening of a young mind, and a friendship that spans generations."
— *The Globe and Mail*

"I had absolutely no idea how enjoyable a journey it would be meandering through the 219 pages of this touching yarn of a boy and his grandfather, their mutual love of baseball and, in particular, the game's greatest performer, George Herman Ruth, a.k.a. The Bambino."
— *The Toronto Sun*

"*Gift of the Bambino* will hold your interest from the prologue through to the final page and the entire trip can be best described as a wonderful surprise."
— Sean Holtz, Baseball Almanac Newsletter,
Society for American Baseball Research

"The subtitle of this book should really be 'baseball as a metaphor for life'. A boy and a grandfather form a close relationship owing to their common love of baseball. The plot revolves around Babe Ruth's first home run in 1914 and the quest for the remains of that magical ball."
— *Library Journal*

"The Toronto rookie novelist has created a captivating tale of baseball and life in bittersweet notes."
— *The Seattle Post-Intelligencer*

"Fantasy and fact are woven together seamlessly in *Gift of the Bambino* and the exploration of life's relationships through baseball are warm and timeless."
— Baseball Almanac

BABE RUTH

A SUPERSTAR'S LEGACY

Jerry Amernic

To Geoffrey,

Jerry Amernic

Wordcraft Communications

© 2018 Jerry Amernic

ISBN 978-1-7752399-0-1

www.BabeRuthLegacy.com

Cover and text design by Tania Craan

Wordcraft Communications
341 Beechgrove Drive
Toronto, ON M1E 4A2

Printed in Canada

www.jerryamernic.com

*"May the divine spirit that animated
Babe Ruth to win the crucial game of life
inspire the youth of America."*
— *Cardinal Francis Spellman*

Contents

———

Foreword

by Tom Stevens

Although I am not old enough to have met him, Babe Ruth has enriched my life and that of my family immeasurably. I'm not referring to monetary riches. Not only was the Babe generous to a fault, but he willed all his memorabilia to the National Baseball Hall of Fame and Museum, the only inductee we are aware of to do so. Had he not possessed the foresight to purchase some annuities during his playing days, his short-lived retirement could have been far different. It is a fact that many of his contemporaries retired to a life of virtual poverty. No, rather than money, it is his legacy that my family and I benefit from.

Growing up as his grandson has afforded us the opportunity to meet U.S. presidents, movie stars, and star athletes. I like to think of it as having had the good fortune to be born into baseball royalty. For my part, I have always considered it to be nothing less than an honor and privilege.

I cannot remember a time when he was not a significant part of my life, and at a young age, I began to realize that this guy was something special.

I think it was around 1958 or '59 that my grandmother Claire, my mother Julia, and I were invited to appear on Edward R. Murrow's television show 'Person to Person.' Unlike today, television programming at the time was quite limited, so to appear on TV was a pretty big deal. (Edward R. Murrow was a pioneering, Grammy Award-winning, broadcast journalist and one-time vice president at CBS who was noted for his honesty and integrity. He was a prominent character in George Clooney's 2005 Oscar-nominated film 'Good Night, and Good Luck.')

As time passed and I grew older, it became evident that Babe Ruth was a good deal more than just special. Most knowledgeable baseball people of all capacities, including players, managers, and executives, considered him the greatest ballplayer ever, and by a considerable margin at that. But what I heard about from my family, particularly my grandmother and mother, was about Babe the husband and father. How during his playing days, my mother would hold his feet while he did sit-ups at night before going to bed. How he carved the Thanksgiving turkey with his own special flair, or how he would painstakingly drape icicles on the Christmas tree by himself, one by one, late into the night long after the rest of the family had gone to bed. Their recollections and stories have painted a picture for me of a kind and caring man who made sure he was there for his family and friends, and quite often even for complete strangers who were in need.

There is one point I am anxious to clarify for readers — the Babe had his appetites to be sure, and this was well documented over the years. This endeared him, in part, to some of his many fans. But it is infuriating when people dwell on the alcohol and women, especially when it had little to do with his ability to play baseball, nor did it have the slightest impact. If he drank to the extent, or spent as much time with the ladies as the media would have you believe, he would have had barely enough time to play ball, let alone excel in the manner that he did.

In 1902, when he was still a small child at the age of seven and growing up completely unsupervised in the bowery of Baltimore, he came to the attention of social services. Recognizing that he was terribly neglected and not receiving the parenting that he needed, social workers recommended that he be placed in an environment where he would receive adequate guidance. Unsure of what else to do with him, his parents promptly deposited him at St. Mary's Industrial School (not orphanage) to learn the trade of tailoring. This child would never again know any real love or affection, other than what was administered by the Xaverian brothers at St. Mary's, until he was a grown man with his own family.

Twelve years later when he was nineteen, Jack Dunn, the manager of the then minor-league Baltimore Orioles, assumed guardianship for him so that he could leave St. Mary's to begin his baseball career. Consider that to this point in his life, he had never tasted a steak, ridden a bicycle, or even ridden in an elevator. Barely two years later at the age of twenty-one, he was a rising star with the Red Sox, the toast of America, and on his way to becoming the best left-handed pitcher in the American League. Everyone wanted to meet him, be his friend, or be able to say that they bought him a drink. He was being offered the world and everything in it. Especially given his underprivileged upbringing, who under the same circumstances would not embrace life and all that it had to offer?

After his disastrous year in 1925 (for him), many thought he was washed up, his career over at age thirty. He "only" hit .290 with 25 home runs. While a sub-par year for him, it was nonetheless a year that many lesser ballplayers would be quite happy with. But we are talking about Babe Ruth, and even he realized that he could not continue to burn the candle at both ends. So he resolved to turn his life around and even retained a personal trainer for the remainder of his career. To the best of our knowledge, he was the first professional athlete to do so. Sure enough, not only did he have a stellar year in 1926 (.372 batting average with 47 home runs), he continued to excel for almost another decade. Sixty home runs, Called Shots, and many milestones that would stand for decades were still ahead. He was just getting started and hadn't shown them anything yet.

My profession as a civil engineer has taken me overseas to reside and work in many countries that do not care one iota about the game of baseball. Nonetheless, to my continual surprise, the Babe is still well known, even in the developing world. Two weeks after moving to

Thailand, I encountered his picture hanging on a restaurant wall in a country club. A few weeks later, I found a picture of him bowling that I had never seen before in a restaurant in Bangkok.

Hands down, the greatest batsman of all time in the sport of cricket is an Australian named Sir Don Bradman. As his name states, he was knighted by Queen Elizabeth for his many accomplishments, but in his home country he is known as 'The Babe Ruth of cricket.'

While overseeing the design and construction of strategic bridges for the U.S. military in Uruzgan Province, Afghanistan, I learned that the South African paramilitary personnel providing superb security for my bridge sites 24/7 were not only familiar with the Babe, they were fans.

A few years ago, the Monaco branch of British banking giant Barclays sought the family's permission to use one of the Babe's famous quotes for their portfolio management group. (In 1930, during the height of the Depression, he signed a two-year contract for $80,000 per year. Sportswriters asked how he could justify commanding a salary exceeding that of President Herbert Hoover. His response was, "I had a better year." It has perhaps become cliché to say, but clearly his celebrity has come to transcend baseball.

It has now been more than eighty years since he last played baseball, and to our continuing wonder and delight, public fascination with him is perhaps as great as it has ever been. Learning about my grandfather and coming to know him is a journey upon which I embarked while still in grammar school, and it continues to this day. I am continually discovering something new as I did while reading *Babe Ruth — A Superstar's Legacy* by Jerry Amernic, which is the first real effort to explain his enduring popularity. He started from absolutely nothing and grew up to be hosted by royalty, presidents, and the most important people of his time. He was, and still is, the very embodiment of the American dream.

I hope readers of *Babe Ruth — A Superstar's Legacy* will enjoy it just as I did, and come away with a fondness and appreciation for this true American hero who gave us so much more than baseball exploits alone.

Tom Stevens and his mother Julia Ruth Stevens, daughter of
Babe Ruth, wave to fans at the very last game at the original Yankee
Stadium which was known as 'The House that Ruth built.' The stadium
had opened in 1923. Julia threw out the game ball for the last game
on September 21, 2008. She was ninety-two at the time.

Introduction

IT TURNED OUT to be one of those days when it was just plain good luck or maybe predestination that reared its head for me. I was taking in a reunion dinner for this group called the Lizzies and there were perhaps two hundred gentlemen in the room. All of them elderly. It was supposed to be research for what would be my first novel — *Gift of the Bambino* — a coming-of-age story about a young boy and his grandfather, and how their lives were bound by baseball and the spirit of Babe Ruth.

The Lizzies were an organization of boys' sports teams in the City of Toronto and it was a popular group for the first half of the 20th century. My Dad was a member of the Lizzies himself. After he died I discovered his team photo from 1934, when he was fifteen years old. It was a basketball team of all things and they were the city's bantam champions that year. He was standing in the back row wearing no. 3.

The Babe's number.

Strangely enough, to this day that remains the only photo I have ever seen of him as a boy, but it served me in good stead as it would be the catalyst for what ultimately became the novel.

I remember the evening well. The guest speaker that night was none other than boxer George Chuvalo, who in his prime was one of the top-ranked heavyweights in the world. He once went fifteen rounds with Muhammad Ali without getting knocked down. And so, there I was with these men, strangers all, seated at tables in this big banquet hall and every one of them had a good thirty or forty years on me.

The man next to me wondered what someone my age was doing there and I told him I was doing research on the Lizzies for a book I was writing.

"What's your book about?" he asked.

"Oh, it's about baseball ... and Babe Ruth," I said.

"Hmm," he said with a shrug and then out it came.

"I knew Babe Ruth."

He didn't say it in a boastful way or any particular way. He said it how someone would say that they know Joe Smith or Mary Brown.

"Excuse me? You *knew* Babe Ruth?"

"Yes. I was with the Brooklyn Dodgers in 1938 and he had the locker next to me in the team dressing room."

Talk about good fortune but of all the men in that room I just happened to sit down beside Goody Rosen. At the time I didn't even know who Goody Rosen was. Sure, he had been a Lizzie just like everyone else in the place, but Goody Rosen was also the only person there that night who had been a Major League Baseball player. And a pretty good one, too.

Back in 1938 he was a rookie with the Brooklyn Dodgers. For the next ten years he would bounce back and forth between the majors and minors. But he was a major-league regular for six seasons and in 1945 he was the third-leading hitter in the National League with a .325 batting average. For a time that season he was even flirting with the league's batting crown.

I once met the late sportswriter Robert W. Creamer, who penned what most people in the know consider the best biography ever done on Babe Ruth. That would be *Babe — The Legend Comes to Life* (Simon & Schuster, New York 1974). I happened to mention my chance encounter with Rosen and Creamer said right away: "Goody Rosen was a good ballplayer."

Indeed, throughout his career Rosen had to contend with three knocks against him. First, he was small for a baseball player even back in the Depression era when he first came up, and players then were miniscule compared to today. Rosen stood 5'9" and weighed all of 155 pounds. Second, he was a Canadian and there were only a handful of them in the majors at the time. One who had made his debut three seasons before Rosen was George 'Twinkletoes' Selkirk, a native of Huntsville, Ontario. He had the misfortune of being the man to succeed Babe Ruth in the Yankees outfield after the Yanks had granted Ruth his release to join the Boston Braves of the National League. If that wasn't bad enough, Selkirk would also be given Ruth's no. 3 which didn't get retired until 1948, the year the Babe died.

The third knock about Rosen was that he was Jewish, and maybe all these things are what made him 'scrappy' because that's what people tend to say about him. But as it turned out, Rosen did pretty well for himself. The first Canadian ever named to a major league All-Star Team, he once said that his proudest accomplishment was being the only Jewish Canadian to play in the majors. That would be the case until 2005 when Adam Stern, who is from London, Ontario, joined the Boston Red Sox.

As for Ruth, in 1938 it was just three years after his retirement as a player. That season he was signed by the Brooklyn Dodgers as a coach. It was a publicity stunt, but at the time he was still hoping to be a manager somewhere and to him this looked like a good opportunity. After all, Dodgers' manager Burleigh Grimes had made it known that he wouldn't be coming back the next season, so Ruth was offered $15,000 — not an insignificant sum in 1938 — to put on a team uniform and show all the fans he was really there. Ruth, more than portly by this time, even took batting and fielding practice, played in some exhibition games, and served as the first-base coach in regular-season games. Everybody liked him except Leo Durocher, the Dodger shortstop and team captain.

Ruth told stories on the bench and was known to make a lot of noise in the clubhouse. That same Robert W. Creamer got into this in his Ruth biography. During that 1938 season, according to Creamer, Burleigh Grimes said that everyone on the team listened whenever Ruth spoke, everyone except Durocher, who as it turned out would succeed Grimes as Dodgers' manager the next season. As I discovered later, my newfound friend Goody Rosen didn't have much affinity for Durocher either, but he thought the world of Ruth.

"I was just a rookie and he had me look after his humidor," Rosen told me. "You know? For his cigars."

Well, that night at the Lizzies' reunion dinner Goody Rosen went on about Babe Ruth this and Babe Ruth that. Rosen died in 1994 and when I saw his obituary in the newspaper — the headline was *Canadian baseball great 'Goody' Rosen dies at 81* — I fondly recalled my evening with him and our chat about his old buddy the Babe.

Rosen was no slouch as a ballplayer. After being called up to the Dodgers in September, 1937, he appeared in twenty-two games and made an immediate impression with his .312 batting average. The next season, his first full one in the majors, he hit .281 and led all National League outfielders with a .989 fielding percentage and nineteen assists. That year he played 138 games, handled 285 chances, and made only three errors.

Later in his career, after spending four years in the minors, he was back with the Dodgers and wanted a raise after his vintage 1945 season. But he didn't get along with manager Durocher and he didn't get that raise either. The Dodgers' star outfielder Pete Reiser had just returned from his stint in the army, so Rosen was sold to the New York Giants for two players and $50,000. In his big-league career, Rosen played a total of 551 games and posted a very respectable lifetime batting average of .291.

Here was a guy who had always been told that he was too small to play, that he would never make it, and he proved them wrong. In 1984 he was inducted into the Canadian Baseball Hall of Fame.

One thing Rosen said about Babe Ruth in our talk that night has stuck with me through the years and I remember it like it was yesterday. After realizing that this chance encounter with someone who intimately knew Babe Ruth was really happening, I had grabbed a pen and notepad and started scribbling down everything he was telling me.

"I understand he was quite a rabble-rouser," I had said at one point in the conversation, recalling the many stories that had been associated with Ruth.

Rosen replied with a nod. "Oh yes he was." And then, under his breath, so quietly you almost couldn't hear it, he offered his summary of Babe Ruth.

"He was a good person though."

This is something I would learn with every individual I talked to about Babe Ruth over the next twenty-five years.

Chapter 1

THE ENIGMA

This drawing of Babe Ruth by William Auerbach-Levy
made circa 1929 involves gouache, graphite and ink on paper,
and was part of the Babe Ruth exhibit at the National Portrait
Gallery at the Smithsonian Institution in Washington, D. C.

A NY BUILDING DEDICATED to history and greatness must be some-thing special, and the one in Washington, D. C. housing the National Portrait Gallery and Smithsonian American Art Museum fills the bill. It was once called "that noblest of Washington buildings" by none other than Walt Whitman. The grandiose edifice, which began as the Old Patent Office Building, is the third oldest public building in the city. The only ones older are the Capitol and the White House.

It covers an entire city block and is teeming with history. Soldiers were billeted there during the Civil War and Abraham Lincoln cele-brated his second inaugural in its Great Hall. Today, more than one million people come through the doors every year to attend exhibi-tions, performances and other programs.

Pierre Charles L'Enfant, the military engineer who designed the basic plan for the nation's capital in the late 1700s, had in mind a structure that would be devoted to great Americans. Construction didn't actually begin until 1836 and it would take thirty-one years before the thing was done.

In 1953 there was a move to demolish the building for a park-ing lot, of all things, but the president at the time — Dwight D. Eisenhower — would have none of that. He signed legislation that would give the building to the Smithsonian. In 1965 the building was designated a National Historic Landmark and three years later it opened as the National Collection of Fine Arts (later renamed the Smithsonian American Art Museum) and the National Portrait Gallery. The north wing would house the art museum and the south wing the portrait gallery.

At the turn of the last century — we are talking the year 2000 — a major and very costly renovation required the building to be closed for six full years. But on July 1, 2006, it reopened for the 230th birthday of the United States.

Since that reopening the National Portrait Gallery has been holding special exhibits as part of the One Life series which dedicates an entire gallery in the building to the biography of a single person. The intent is to focus on the life and influence of that particular individual. Over the years the One Life series has featured a short list — very short — of Americans worthy of inclusion. The list includes three presidents — Abraham Lincoln, Ulysses S. Grant, and Ronald Reagan — and a noted military man, Confederate General Robert E. Lee from the Civil War days. It also includes Washington Post publisher Katherine Graham who forged her reputation with the Watergate investigation, civil rights leader Martin Luther King Jr., labor leader and civil rights activist Dolores Huerta, the aforementioned poet and essayist Walt Whitman, singer Elvis Presley, and Thomas Paine who was one of the Founding Fathers of the United States.

But from June 24, 2016 to May 21, 2017, the One Life series was about someone else from an altogether different walk of life than those people. Babe Ruth. Here is what the Smithsonian had to say about the exhibit in its news release from May 31, 2016:

> "This exhibition examines Babe Ruth as a baseball legend and the marketing frenzy his name and image fueled before the commercialization of sports superstars became routine. Related themes focus on star power in an age before electronic mass media and the use of portraiture in advertising. The photographic record alone is astonishing. Ruth was arguably the most portrayed American from the beginning of his professional career in the major leagues, in 1914, to his death in 1948. No president, Hollywood star, or athlete so enjoyed the limelight for as long as Babe Ruth."

The exhibit had more than thirty items depicting Ruth in prints and photographs. There was an iconic photo of him in his New York Yankees uniform from 1927, the bat perched on his shoulder, his face all business. Of course, 1927 was the year he hit sixty home runs and that Yankees team is still regarded as the best in history. There was a 1915 photo of the five starting pitchers from the Boston Red Sox. Ruth was only twenty then, the youngest starter on the team and just one year removed from the beginning of his professional baseball career. During the 1915 season he became a pitching sensation with an 18-8 won-loss record. The Red Sox won the World Series that year with him on the team, and would do it again in 1916 and yet again in 1918.

There was a caricature drawing that made the cover of *Time* magazine from April 26, 1976 with the opening of the newly refurbished Yankee Stadium. The drawing depicted a giant Ruth sitting on the roof of the stadium, his legs crossed, one hand scratching his temple and the other resting on his bat, the masses clamoring to get in under his feet.

This was twenty-eight years after the man's death.

There was the famous photograph of an ailing Ruth, taken from the back, by photographer Nat Fein. It had been shot on June 13, 1948, the day that Ruth made his last visit to Yankee Stadium. The following year this photo would win Fein the Pulitzer Prize.

The exhibit also included a caricature of Ruth that made the cover of *Vanity Fair* from 1933, a photograph showing him surrounded by a sea of admiring boys, another photo with a string of Hollywood starlets on either side of him, not to mention a number of novelty items — everything from Babe Ruth Comics to a wrapper for Ruth's Home Run chocolate-coated candy.

According to the Smithsonian, the idea behind the One Life series is to tell the multifaceted story of America "through the individuals who have shaped its culture." Babe Ruth was a baseball player who was born in 1895, played his last major-league game in 1935, and died in 1948. Along the way he hit 714 home runs, but that is almost beside the point because with Babe Ruth we are talking about an enigma whose orbit and impact went far beyond baseball. Indeed, Babe Ruth transcended not only baseball but sport, entertainment, and even America itself.

He transcended everything, and with all due respect to those who were the subjects of earlier exhibits in the One Life series, there has never been anyone quite like him in the history of the United States.

When the exhibit opened he had been dead for sixty-eight years, and while it is possible that a handful of visitors might have seen him play, it's fair to assume that almost all who came knew him from what they had heard or read or maybe from what they had seen in movies and old film clips. And make no mistake, they have heard, read and seen a lot.

James Barber is a historian and curator of the National Portrait Gallery and is the person who first proposed that the One Life series do an exhibit on Ruth. In a statement promoting the exhibit he said: "As big and bright as his celebrity star was, his natural disposition was to be one of us which is what I find most interesting about Babe Ruth."

The One Life series is always held in one room — four walls — to showcase the featured items. Portraiture is supposed to be the thing. Barber points out that there were tens of thousands, if not hundreds of thousands, of photographs taken of Ruth during his time and that

Babe Ruth exhibit at the National Portrait Gallery at the Smithsonian

the exhibit tried to capture different aspects of his life from that multitude of photographs and prints.

Says Barber: "I've always been intrigued by him and the fact is anytime is a good time to do Babe Ruth. He led a Horatio Alger kind of life and was one of the most portrayed Americans of his generation. I've been doing this for a long time and two personalities stand out — Theodore Roosevelt and Babe Ruth. Each of them led three lives and there will never be others like them because of what they accomplished. With Teddy Roosevelt his writing alone would have been a career for most people. He was a public servant, a writer and an adventurer, but he only lived to sixty so with him it's not the number but the mileage. Babe Ruth is the other one and for him it's not that number 714. In fact, he broke the home-run record 576 times because his record stood for so long."

What were the three lives of Babe Ruth? Barber says those three lives were his baseball career, his home and social life, and his secret personal life which in those days was kept out of the public eye. How special was he?

Babe Ruth exhibit at the National Portrait Gallery at the Smithsonian

"Babe Ruth's name is still universally known around the world," Barber says.

End of story.

That profound statement comes from a man who is a respected historian and scholar. Barber has a Master's degree in history from the Virginia Polytechnic Institute & State University, and is an acknowledged expert on the portraiture of Andrew Jackson and the Civil War. He has spent years doing research on the American presidency. He was an editorial consultant for the Smithsonian book *The Civil War: A Visual History*, and the curator of two Portrait Gallery exhibitions that commemorate the 150th anniversary of the Civil War. He is also curator of the Portrait Gallery's *Time* collection which includes more than 2,000 original works of art that have appeared on the covers of *Time* magazine. Barber has organized biographical exhibitions about Theodore Roosevelt, George C. Marshall, Ulysses S. Grant, and Andrew Jackson. His publications include *Theodore Roosevelt: Icon of the American Century, George C. Marshall: Soldier of Peace, Andrew Jackson: A Portrait Study, and Faces of Discord: The Civil War at the National Portrait Gallery.*

An expert on presidents, war heroes, and American history, James Barber says Babe Ruth just may be the most universally known American name in the world.

Ruth's story — the legend and the reality, and the two are so interwoven that it's often hard to tell where one ends and the other begins — naturally started in the United States. We can go back to 1920 when the baseball world was stunned with his trade from the Boston Red Sox to the New York Yankees. The deal involved over $100,000 — a huge sum at the time, especially for a baseball player. The summer before, in 1919, Ruth then with the Red Sox, had set a new home-run record with twenty-nine dingers. Fast-forward almost a century later to 2014. A promissory note — a bank issue — dated December 30, 1919 in the amount of $25,000 from the Royal Bank of Canada, which was one of the financial institutions involved in that historic transaction, sold at auction for $151,250.

That was a lot of money for a slip of paper, but peanuts compared to what a New York Yankees jersey worn by Ruth in the early 1920s had sold for two years earlier — in 2012. That occurred in another auction. The jersey sold for *$4.4 million*, which incredible as it may seem, was almost twice what it cost to build the original Yankee Stadium in 1923! What's more, the $4.4 million was a new world record for an item of sports memorabilia and still stands today, as recognized by Guinness World Records.

What might be even more remarkable is this. The Yankees jersey and Ruth are anything but a one-time thing. Items that feature Babe Ruth in any way — a signature, an article of clothing he had worn, a photograph — usually fetch a lot of money, much more money than for any other baseball player, any other athlete, and any other person.

Lists about the most expensive pieces of sports memorabilia ever sold are constantly changing, but one list compiled in early 2017 concluded that seven of the fifteen most expensive pieces of sports memorabilia ever sold — for any sport in the world, anywhere in the world, and any athlete in the world — were Babe Ruth items. The old Yankees jersey was at the top of the ladder.

The business of sports memorabilia is big and growing every year. It involves many sports and people from all around the globe. Babe Ruth is not only no. 1 in the industry, but the gap between him and other pretenders to the throne keeps widening. If you like to invest in things that will appreciate over time, Babe Ruth just might be a better game to play than real estate or the stock market.

He might be better than gold.

In 2015 Leaf Trading Cards — a company that produces trading cards and sports collectibles — signed a deal with the estate of Babe Ruth to make Ruth items available to the masses through such retailers as Walmart and Target. Why? The CEO of the company said there were three reasons they did this: there will never be another Babe Ruth, the man was larger than life, and the deal means you can get a history lesson from a box of trading cards.[1]

It is now seven decades after Ruth's passing and his legacy is stronger than ever. More than one million kids and youths play in a league that bears his name — Babe Ruth League — and another two million people serve as volunteers for that league. That makes a total of three million people which would constitute a sizeable city. Babe Ruth League Baseball got going in the early 1950s with the impetus of Ruth's widow Claire, his second wife, and is one of the biggest sports organizations in the world.

Today Babe Ruth's name is worth multi-millions in endorsement appeal and his grave is hallowed ground. No one would dream of digging up his bones, as they did with Charlie Chaplin, or freezing his remains à la Ted Williams. This is Babe Ruth we're talking about and the word *sacrilege* comes to mind.

This is a man who exemplifies what America is all about. A Rocky Balboa character of Paul Bunyan-like dimensions who never forgot where he came from, he was common, raw and unspoilt, and deeply loved by his legions of admirers. He is indelibly entwined with the very fabric of America and today he sits on a pedestal that is higher than ever. Not only is he indestructible as an icon, but as time marches on he keeps getting bigger and bigger.

He was a man of mythological proportions who happened to come along at the right time in the right place. The Roaring Twenties, New York City and Babe Ruth were indeed the Perfect Storm for building a legend and he remains an integral character — a fixture — in American culture. He and his brand are a most unique phenomenon in terms of star power, inspiration and sheer public appeal.

There have been many books about Babe Ruth — biographies, anthologies, fantasies, children's books, books with photos and memorabilia. Two films were made about his life — *The Babe Ruth Story* in 1948 and *The Babe* in 1992 — and talk about sacrilege but having such physically clumsy, rotund actors as William Bendix (1948) and John Goodman (1992) portray a man like Ruth, whose pure athleticism and eye-hand coordination were off the charts, would

Babe Ruth exhibit at the National Portrait Gallery at the Smithsonian

be paramount to having someone of Woody Allen's dimensions and physical skills masquerade as Muhammad Ali.

But the thing about Babe Ruth lasting through the ages goes beyond sport and beyond his accomplishments as an athlete, considerable as they are. Ruth the man plays a part, too. A very big part.

He was both a humanitarian and a pioneer in the truest sense of those words. Babe Ruth encouraged the players of his day to stand up for their rights against unscrupulous owners. What's more, he played baseball with blacks when it wasn't done. In World War II prominent Americans of German heritage signed their names to full-page ads in some of the country's biggest newspapers condemning the Nazi regime, and Ruth was the most prominent name of all.

He wasn't only the first baseball or sports superstar, but the first superstar period. And while others may come and go, he has remained one ever since.

At the National Baseball Hall of Fame and Museum, Babe Ruth is still the top attraction. He is the most prominent player seen on posters adorning storefronts of the main street of Cooperstown, New York, and is one of only two ballplayers with their own exhibits, the other being Henry Aaron. Today his likeness is plastered everywhere in that fabled town, and Hall of Fame guide books and brochures feature him above all others.

That might be what first attracted him to an Indiana lawyer who would become CEO and Chairman of CMG Worldwide, a company that acts as the representative of celebrities and their estates. In the early 1980s Mark Roesler decided to build a career representing the estates and families of dead celebrities — *delebs* they are called — and three of the first ones he would represent were Elvis Presley, James Dean and Babe Ruth. Today the business side of Ruth is handled by another company, The Luminary Group, and no surprise but Ruth reigns as its major brand.

Then there are the monuments, statues and plaques erected and posted across America and in other countries around the world. In Japan he continues to be worshipped as the most popular, if not *the* most significant person, the United States has ever produced.

But, of course, the love is strongest in America. The Babe Ruth Birthplace and Museum in Baltimore is established in the very tene-ment house where he was born. Not far away is a colossal, sixteen-foot bronze likeness of Ruth at Camden Yards, home of the American League Baltimore Orioles. Did the man ever play for Baltimore's major-league team? No. But he was born in the city and that is enough.

The only other statues of such massive size honoring real-life Americans are reserved for a select few: George Washington, Thomas Jefferson, Ulysses S. Grant, Martin Luther King, Marilyn Monroe, Hiowatha, and Texas politician Sam Houston. That makes four poli-ticians of whom three were presidents. One was an African American civil rights leader, one was a movie star, and one was a Native American.

And one was Babe Ruth, this multi-dimensional curiosity of a baseball player. But then he was so much more than that.

The February 1995 issue of *The Smithsonian Magazine* had an article by sportswriter Robert W. Creamer whose 1974 book *Babe — The Legend Comes to Life* (Simon & Schuster, 1974) is widely regarded as the best biography ever written about Ruth. His article was titled 'Rutholatry, or why everyone loves the Babe' and it made the point that forty-six years after the man's death he was still going strong. Creamer, who passed away in 2012, began his article like this:

> 'It is now more than 46 years since Babe Ruth died. In May it will be 60 years since he played his last big league game. Baseball's popularity has risen and fallen in the decades since, and heroes have come and gone. Yet every day Babe Ruth's name pops up on radio or television, in newspaper columns and magazine stories, in casual conversation.'

In the piece Creamer said that Roger Maris, whose victorious assault on Ruth's home-run record in 1961 captivated America, "had receded into the shadows." Of Henry Aaron, who had broken Ruth's all-time home-run record in 1974, Creamer wrote: "But you don't hear Aaron's name every day, you don't feel his presence."

Not so with Ruth. "He is still in the spotlight, still going strong," said Creamer.

And why is that? In addition to all the baseball exploits was something that this writer, who may have been as familiar with the phenomenon of Babe Ruth as anyone, candidly observed. It had to do with duty and responsibility. Creamer said that despite his carefree ways, "Ruth almost always retained a sense of obligation to his role as hero" and maintained that to the very end of his life. When Ruth was near death in 1948, he left his hospital room and flew to Baltimore to appear at a charity game, but it was rained out. He also left hospital one more time after that when asked to attend the premiere of the movie *The Babe Ruth Story*, so he went but had to leave early because he was so ill.

Said Creamer in his article: "He was the best baseball player who ever lived. He was better than Ty Cobb, better than Joe DiMaggio, better than Ted Williams, better than Willie Mays, better than Henry Aaron, better than Barry Bonds. He was by far the most flamboyant. There's never been anyone else like him. And that, I suppose, is why people talk about Babe Ruth all the time."

Fast-forward to the year 2006 when the same Creamer would do another piece, this time for website www.hofmag.com. The article was called 'Why Babe Ruth Still Matters.' Barry Bonds had just passed Ruth on the all-time, home-run list and Creamer acknowledged that it didn't matter because Ruth was still *King of the Home Run.* Wrote Creamer:

> 'Bonds wasn't setting a new record by passing Ruth. All he was doing was moving into second place, still 50 homers behind Aaron. Barry's own TV show on ESPN, "Bonds on Bonds," bombed and was cancelled. Critics commented on Barry's lack of personal appeal. Yet there was Ruth, still everywhere, still center stage.'

Why? Creamer concluded that the key to all this was that Ruth *'spread joy and pleasure wherever he went. He was fun to be around, fun to watch.'* [2]

Today his solemn grave at Gate of Heaven cemetery in Hawthorne, New York is sacred soil. It is a holy place — a truly *American* holy place — that is always adorned with Yankee caps, baseballs, and letters from people who bring their personal messages to the Babe. Even if they were born many decades after his death. They tuck their notes under the corner of his monument or plant them in the dirt in much the same way that people slip letters into the cracks of the Western Wall in Jerusalem. Yes, it is like that. And why?

They haven't forgotten.

"There was just one ... one Babe Ruth ...
and there will never be another one."
— *Julia Ruth Stevens*

Chapter 2

———

DADDY'S GIRL

S HE IS THE ONLY ONE who remains from the Babe Ruth household of those halcyon New York City days in the 1920s and 1930s when he was the most famous person in America and maybe, the entire world. Julia Ruth Stevens — she turned 101 in the summer of 2017 — is the daughter of Babe Ruth. She isn't his biological daughter, mind you. That would be too simple, too logical, and there isn't much that is simple or logical about this man and what he has left behind.

Back in his heyday with the New York Yankees, Ruth was head of a family that included his second wife Claire, Claire's daughter Julia, Claire's mother, two of her brothers, and a younger daughter Dorothy who had been adopted by Ruth and his first wife Helen. Dorothy died in 1989, leaving Julia as the only person remaining from that group.

Now into her second century, Julia is not as sturdy as a few years ago when she could still be counted on to do things because of who she is. However, as recently as 2016 she did appear at Fenway Park in Boston to throw out the first pitch at a Red Sox game in honor of her 100th birthday. And two years earlier, in 2014, she had taken part at an event in St. Petersburg, Florida. It was held to recognize 100 years of professional baseball in the community and spring training in St. Petersburg. Incidentally, the Babe is said to have hit the first 500-foot home run while in spring training with the Boston Red Sox. He was a young starring pitcher at the time. They say the ball travelled 573 feet. Maybe more.

It happened in Hot Springs, Arkansas on March 17, 1918. The Red Sox were there for spring training and it was an exhibition game. One hundred years later in March, 2018, an event would be held in Hot Springs to commemorate that homer.

As for the New York Yankees, St. Pete's was something of a home for them, too. From 1925 to 1961, minus a few breaks in between, St. Pete's was where the Yankees held their annual spring training, and when Julia was a young girl she even went to school there. Every spring multitudes of tourists would pour into town to see the Yankees and, of course, the Babe.

Today Julia resides in an assisted-living facility in Nevada outside Las Vegas, where her son Tom and his wife Anita live. The family still owns the house which Julia had bought in 1965 in a small town in northern New Hampshire just inside the border with Maine. The community, a year-round tourist town that attracts skiers and sun-seekers, goes all the way back to 1765 which means that it pre-dates American independence.

Julia got the name 'Ruth' when her mother Claire, who was a young widow at the beginning of the Roaring Twenties, married her second husband. The Babe. The marriage didn't take place until the end of that most turbulent of decades, in 1929, but by then Babe was already a fixture in her life. His relationship with Claire began in 1922 when Julia was six and he was the only 'Daddy' she ever knew. He adopted her, gave her away when she got married, and the two remained close until his death in 1948.

She still suffers from it. His death. Even now. More than seven decades have passed since that fateful day and the hurt is still on her face whenever the subject is raised. The contrast between the sorrow she wears and the obvious joy she exudes when speaking of all the memories is nothing short of profound.

Julia, the daughter of Babe Ruth, has been getting around with a walker since breaking her hip in a fall, and while she calls herself 'disabled' and doesn't get out much anymore, when something involving 'Daddy' comes up she tries not to disappoint. She was well into her 90s when she threw out the game ball at the very last game at Yankee Stadium — *old* Yankee Stadium, The House That Ruth Built. And in 2010, she flew with her grandson Brent to Boise, Idaho to be feted by the Sports Humanitarian Hall of Fame for the Babe's induction. There were all those orphanages, hospitals, schools and prisons he had visited when starring with the Yankees, not to mention the Red Sox, and he had even paid for medical operations out of his own pocket when families couldn't afford the tab. He did those things and people never knew.

It was known that he gave money away, and depending on whom you talk to, he may have been an easy mark. But if he was an easy mark there was good reason; this was a man who genuinely cared about people. In 1927, the year he hit those sixty home runs, he helped establish the American Legion Crippled Children's Hospital in St. Petersburg, Florida, which was just one of countless charities he had helped in the community. During World War II — years after his retirement — he got involved with the Red Cross and made a point of visiting military hospitals.

There is much more to Babe Ruth than mere baseball player, albeit the best ever. And who says he is the best ever? Well, just about everyone, including the young. A national telephone survey conducted in 2017 among a national sample of Americans aged eighteen and over by DraftKings Inc., a big player in the fantasy sports business, found that more than 40% of respondents said Ruth was the best baseball player of all time. No one else was even close. No other player got even one-tenth of the support garnered by Ruth. Jackie Robinson and Mickey Mantle each claimed 4%. The threesome of Henry Aaron, Willie Mays and Derek Jeter each claimed 3%, while four players — Joe DiMaggio, Pete Rose, Ken Griffey, Jr., and Lou Gehrig — each got 2%.

What is most interesting about the survey, however, is that the greatest percentage of Americans who selected Ruth were Millennials, those born between 1982 and 2004. Some 48% of them opted for Ruth.[3]

He was a superstar, the first one, in fact. He is the man whom they say invented the autograph and paved the way for all who came after him, no matter what walk of life they chose. He was a pioneer who never forgot his humble roots or his admirers even if they didn't know much about baseball. He was worshipped for such things, but the humanitarian bit is special.

When his induction into the Sports Humanitarian Hall of Fame was announced, the organization issued a news release quoting Ford Frick, a former Commissioner of Major League Baseball. Frick once said this of Babe Ruth:

> "Babe Ruth needed every inch of that big chest of his to protect the world's largest heart. I never saw a man with more heart, and you can interpret that as meaning both courage on the field and consideration for others."

When Ruth retired in 1935 he wanted to be a manager, but no one in baseball would hire him. There is a quote that has made the rounds that goes like this: How could Babe Ruth manage a whole team when he couldn't even manage himself? Where it really comes from is up for grabs, but Julia says there is nothing to it. Just hogwash. According to her, and she was there, the owners of the time thought Ruth as a manager would encourage players to ask for more money and that is why no one would hand him a job. Collusion among the owners? Julia tells a story about Lou Gehrig, the Iron Horse, a man she knew very well.

"I remember when Lou came to Daddy and his contract was up and he was going to see [Yankees owner] Col. Ruppert. Lou asked Daddy if he thought he should ask for a raise and Daddy said, 'Good Lord, yes!' I can't remember what he was getting but it was probably somewhere between $15,000 and $18,000 and Daddy said to ask him for $40,000. Lou said, "That much?' And Daddy said you may have to come down a little but make it difficult for the Colonel."

Julia laughs. Her son Tom, who often represents the family for sponsorships and endorsements, concurs and offers yet another plum, and this one is even better. Tom mentions the Babe's barnstorming trips in the offseason when he would take major-league players to tour cities and towns that didn't have teams of their own, and he says Babe often played against top teams in the old Negro leagues. Back in those days, black players weren't allowed to play big-league ball. Baseball was segregated. Ruth taking the field with blacks is a precious tidbit

Babe Ruth signing a contract with Yankees owner
Col. Jacob Ruppert as wife Claire looks on.

that wasn't known at the time, and there is good reason that no one knew. Many white sports writers refused to cover those games. Tom says that Babe even faced the legendary Satchel Paige a few times — and did as well as he did when hitting for the Yankees, thank you very much — but the point is he crossed the color bar when people didn't do such things.

"Babe and the famous tap dancer Bill 'Bojangles' Robinson were friends and in 1932 Babe took him into the Yankee clubhouse," Tom says. "Nobody but Babe could have pulled that off. To bring a person of color to meet all the players. It was met with either shock or out-right hostility. Kenesaw Mountain Landis [Commissioner of Major League Baseball] was aware of that and there is a theory that he may have cautioned owners not to hire Babe as a manager because he would advance the case of black people in baseball."

Shades of Jackie Robinson, and this was long before his time. Just like his mother Julia, Tom also says that the bit about Babe not being able to manage himself is bull.

It's a good story. Babe Ruth, the incorrigible youngster from the wrong side of the tracks, the boy who never grew up, may have been a man ahead of his time. He thought players should get tough in negotiations with the owners, who in his day regarded them as little more than indentured servants. This was when a major-league baseball player was lucky to earn $5,000 a year, and a good forty years before Curt Flood challenged the owners all the way to the U.S. Supreme Court. What's more, Babe never had any qualms about sharing a field with the best black players. He was only interested in baseball.

The Northeast Journal in St. Petersburg is a bi-monthly community newspaper that didn't start publishing until 2004. A regular contributor is Will Michaels, who is not only a writer but a historian with a Ph. D in anthropology. At one time he was Executive Director of the St. Petersburg Museum of History. Michaels is the author of such books as *The Making of St. Petersburg* (The History Press, Charleston SC, 2012) and *Hidden History of St. Petersburg* (The History Press, Charleston SC, 2016).

Michaels did a piece in the March/April 2017 edition of *The Northeast Journal* about Babe Ruth the humanitarian. It mentioned how Ruth had established the Babe Ruth Foundation to help underprivileged children, and how on one of his barnstorming tours in 1918, when he was still with the Red Sox, he had led off the tour with a game against a touring Cuban team that included black players.[4]

His article included a quote from baseball historian Leigh Montville, who wrote the Ruth biography *The Big Bam: The Life and Times of Babe Ruth* (Random House, 2006). Said Montville in the article: "The Babe played with black teams against black teams, with white teams against black teams, and with white teams against white teams. He was a non-denominational, non-discriminatory belter. He played with the old guys against the young guys, with the young guys against the old."

Tim Reid is a baseball historian who helped Michaels with his research on Ruth. He also knows Julia and Tom, and he knows a thing or two about the Babe. In 2008, to mark the 60th anniversary of Ruth's death, he took part in a ceremony at St. Patrick's Cathedral in New York City — the very place where Ruth's funeral mass had been held in 1948. He also helped organize the 2018 event recognizing that monster home run from 1918.

Reid says Ruth was "a 24-hour charity machine" and that in St. Petersburg and around the state of Florida — Ruth was a seasonal resident in St. Pete's for many years — he was involved with at least seventy different charities.

"He didn't like to see people suffer, even his enemies," Reid says and then he served up a long list of organizations such as the John Hopkins Children's Hospital, the YMCA, the Lions Club, girls' clubs and women's clubs, all of which he had helped. "He was an endless fountain of generosity and with no gain for himself. If there was a charity these people came to Babe Ruth for help."

Reid tells the story about how Ruth, when he was with the Yankees, would drive his car up the west side of Manhattan on his way to the Polo Grounds, and later after it was built to Yankee Stadium, and on the way he would stop at such places as the Hebrew Orphanage to lend a hand or just give money away.

In 1959 Babe's widow Claire released the book *The Babe and I* (Prentice-Hall, 1959), which was written with sportswriter Bill Slocum, who had been one of the Babe's ghostwriters. The book was all in first person and many of the things Claire said about her husband are revealing.

'He went to see more sick kids than any man who ever lived. And every visit tore him to pieces. He hated hospitals. And you can imagine some of the sights he saw. He always came home depressed and would sit for hours in a melancholy haze.

'Whenever the Babe made a hospital visit he would find the kids in awe of their hero. He would sit on a bed and in a couple of minutes they'd be all kids together. Once the Babe got them talking the party was on. The kids would climb all over him, kiss him and hug him. And many a kid climbed and hugged who hadn't been able to move his limbs that much in months or years.

'The doctors and the nurses never failed to tell Babe how much good he did. And the Babe never failed to go to his home or his hotel room and sit staring out the window.'[5]

In another passage Claire said this:

'Certainly this is not the first book on Babe Ruth. Much has been written about him. Too much, perhaps. Most of it is junk, although generally harmless junk. The writers wrote of a great and colorful man. They took a lot of baseball statistics, then wrapped them around the fact that he loved kids and sometimes ate too many hot dogs. From that they drew what was purported to be the true picture of a man who is not just a great baseball player, but is, without a doubt, a chapter of Americana that will live in memory long after his baseball records have been surpassed.'[6]

And she told what it was like at the time, which in 1959 was eleven years after he had died:

'I am reminded of my husband a little more often than most widows because I see his name everywhere in the papers, increasingly every year. The legend of the Babe seems to be growing with time. I hear it on the radio and on television. These reminders bring stabs of pain. But they also bring glows of pride.'[7]

Ruth was the first ball player and first athlete anywhere to have an agent and that agent was Christy Walsh. Julia still remembers him well and what she remembers most is that Walsh failed to get the Babe Ruth name trademarked which allowed the Baby Ruth candy bar to make a lot of headway even though it had absolutely nothing to do with 'Daddy.' Babe is also acknowledged as the first athlete to have a personal trainer — Artie McGovern. Having an agent to handle business affairs at a time when no one else did and having a personal trainer to get in shape sure doesn't sound like a man who is incapable of getting his house in order.

The National Baseball Hall of Fame and Museum in Cooperstown, New York features a permanent exhibit for Ruth on the second floor. It has artifacts galore with lots of photographs, but there are also many photos at the family home in New Hampshire, in a room Julia has always called The Den, and there is no doubt whom that room honors. Family photographs are everywhere. There is a wonderful shot of the Babe looking cheerful and dapper in a spanking white suit, and another with a younger Julia and her husband Richard Flanders when they were married in 1940. The two are posing for the camera, along with Babe and Claire, the parents of the bride. It was Babe who gave Julia away that day.

Julia, Babe and Claire in 1936.

Julia at home playing the piano with Babe looking on.

There is a photo from the 1950s with Julia, Tom as a small boy, and an older Claire — Tom's grandmother — and mounted high on the wall between two windows is a spectacular drawing of the Babe. It is two-and-a-half feet long by one-and-a-half feet wide, and the likeness is incredible. A Babe Ruth pillow rests on a chair, a big hunk of crystal with a globe on top sitting on the small side table next to it. That was from the Sports Humanitarian Hall of Fame.

Here we are more than seventy years after Babe Ruth died and more than eighty years after he last appeared in a baseball game, and the accolades are still coming in. Some things don't change. Things like Babe Ruth. His stature keeps on growing.

The last game at old Yankee Stadium was played on September 21, 2008. Escorted by Tom, Julia, then a spry ninety-two, was surely the most seasoned pitcher the park had ever seen. They let her stand closer to the batter's box than the customary sixty feet from the pitcher's mound, but when you're eight years short of a hundred and still get the ball over the plate, it's not bad.

The original building went up in 1923 for one reason and one reason only — to handle the burgeoning crowds that the Babe, the Bambino, was drawing. Go to Cooperstown, at the far end of the hall where all those plaques honoring the members are displayed, and there is a wall reserved for the original five inductees from 1936: Babe Ruth, Ty Cobb, Honus Wagner, Christy Mathewson, Walter Johnson. Ruth's plaque says it all: "Greatest drawing card in history of baseball."

And don't kid yourself, he still is.

Yankee Stadium opened on April 18, 1923, and we all know who hit the first home run. "I was glad to have hit the first home run in this park," said Babe after the game. "God only knows who will hit the last."

It turned out to be Jose Molina, a two-run shot in the fourth inning at that final game. In 2004, the Louisville Slugger bat that Ruth had used to hit the first home run at Yankee Stadium sold for $1.265 million at an auction put on by Sotheby's. Prior to that, the record for a bat was from the collection of 'Shoeless' Joe Jackson, which had gone five years earlier for $577,610. No other baseball bat had ever fetched anywhere near $1 million before, but this is Babe Ruth we are talking about. How much Jose Molina's bat will be worth sixty or seventy years from now we don't know, but one thing is for sure; it will be squat compared to Ruth's.

When that last game at old Yankee Stadium was done, team captain Derek Jeter gave a speech about what an honor it is to wear the uniform every day and how the place holds eighty-five years of tradition, history and memories. Today The House That Ruth Built is gone and for many people — baseball fans and even those who aren't baseball fans — that is a shame. As for the Babe, he is very much alive.

The Babe Ruth League has over one million kids and youths playing on more than 50,000 teams in almost 10,000 leagues across North

America. Julia's mother Claire helped get the Babe Ruth League going not long after his death.

In the world of sports memorabilia, Ruth is unquestionably the hottest commodity around, a veritable gold mine for the sports artifact collector, if not investor. One baseball that he signed fetched almost $400,000. The funny thing about Julia is that she doesn't have any of those valuable baseballs herself. "Who would ask your father for a signed baseball?" she says. "I used to get them for friends but I don't have one. The only signature I ever got was on a check."

The phenomenon of Babe Ruth and his remarkable legacy goes far beyond North America. In 1934 Ruth set Japan on fire when he was one of the American League All-Stars who toured the country. It wasn't the first time the Japanese had seen professional baseball players from the United States in the flesh, but it was the first time they saw Babe Ruth. The cast included his Yankee teammates Lefty Gomez and Lou Gehrig, home run dynamo Jimmie Foxx, and Connie Mack, but Ruth wasn't just another all-star. He was thirty-nine years old at the time, in the twilight of his career, and would never again play for the New York Yankees. Still, he was the main attraction. Julia, who was eighteen, accompanied him on the trip along with her mother Claire. How was he received by the Japanese?

"Like he was a *God*," Julia says. Indeed, upon his arrival the streets of Tokyo were lined with half a million people. Maybe more. A parade was held and he was in one of the cars. Julia tells a story about the man in the hotel.

"We had a suite with two bedrooms and there was a knock on the door. Daddy went to the door and there was a man standing there in a Japanese kimono. They still wore kimonos then. And he said 'sign ball please' and Daddy said sure. He went and got his pen and he signed the ball and then this fellow took another ball out of his kimono. 'Sign ball please.' And Daddy signed that one. And then he pulled another ball out. Daddy would say 'another one?' I think he signed about thirty balls which were hidden in the sleeves of the kimono. It was so funny."

Ruth was a man who was always known to rise to the occasion, and he did in Japan. Despite his age, he was undeniably the MVP for the Americans on the tour and was even awarded two bronze vases by the *Yomiuri Shimbun* newspaper, which had been the sponsor, for his efforts.

There is a biography of Lefty Gomez, Ruth's Yankees teammate who also was on that Japan trip, called *Lefty — An American Odyssey* by Vernona Gomez and Lawrence Goldstone (Ballantine Books, New York 2012). Vernona Gomez was his daughter. The book has a quote from Maye Lazzeri, the wife of Tony Lazzeri who was the no. 2 hitter in the Yankees' famed Murderers' Row lineup, and it refutes what is sometimes written about the wild ways of Babe Ruth.

"It drives me up a wall when sportswriters write all these things about Babe secondhand," Maye Lazzeri said years later. "Babe didn't play ball for all those years and set records because he was a drunk. No alcoholic could play like Babe did. The sportswriters exaggerated everything. It just kills me when they write what a bum he was. Babe was anything but that. He and the whole Yankees club had too much respect for Ruppert [Yankees co-owner Jacob Ruppert] and Barrow [Yankees general manager Ed Barrow] and what the Yankees meant to the fans."[8]

They say Babe Ruth invented the autograph. He was known for obliging the fans and that remains part of the luster, the mystique. His salary peaked at $80,000 in 1930 and he made it for only two seasons. It was a lot of money for the time, but take inflation into account and that translates to about $1 million a season now, or less than what a second-rate player who bounces back and forth between the majors and minors would earn. But no one else commanded that kind of money in those days. Not even close. Ruth was in a class by himself.

After Julia got married, she moved to New Hampshire with her husband. Richard Flanders was a big man, as big as the Babe — the two often played golf together — and he owned the Cranmore Mountain Lodge in New Hampshire. Julia and Richard ran the lodge, a popular place for skiers, until he died suddenly in January, 1949. It was the third death in the family in just over five months; Babe had died in August, 1948, Julia's only remaining uncle the following October, and Richard three months after that.

The proprietor of the Cranmore Mountain Lodge is only too happy to provide a tour of the Babe Ruth Room on the second floor which is available for $134 a night during the week and $154 on the weekend. Breakfast included. The room comes with the same furniture, the same bed, the same dresser he used when he would visit Julia in the 1940s. How often was that? No one really knows. The owner implies that it was frequent, but Julia only says that he stayed there a couple times.

It doesn't matter. He breathed the air and touched things. The furniture is his, the photos on the wall are of him, and downstairs is the Cranmore Mountain Lodge's own version of The Den with Babe Ruth paraphernalia all over the place — family photos, some with Julia and Claire, and a classic shot of Ruth hitting his 60th home run in 1927 and signed in his own hand. *My Sixtieth Homerun.* 'Home run' is spelled as a single word, and one wonders what that signed photo would fetch on the open market. This being Babe Ruth, a man who never got beyond the 8th grade, the spelling error would only enhance its value. The lodge once had a ball signed by Ruth in the downstairs living room, but it was stolen.

Babe Ruth was born on February 6, 1895 (there is some debate about the accuracy of the year) in a tenement house in Baltimore and it wasn't the most auspicious part of town by a long shot. The house has been renovated and is now preserved as the Babe Ruth Birthplace and Museum, a couple streets over from Camden Yards where the Orioles play. Right outside the entrance to the park is a courtyard displaying the numbers of retired Oriole greats — no. 4 Earl Weaver, no. 5 Brooks Robinson, no. 8 Cal Ripken Jr., no. 20 Frank Robinson, no. 22 Jim Palmer, and no. 33 Eddie Murray. Brooks Robinson, who is still regarded by many pundits as the greatest third baseman in history, plied his trade for the Orioles over twenty-three seasons to earn the honor and make no mistake, those aluminum numbers commemorating such Oriole stars are impressive. They stand four feet high, but the statue of the young Babe Ruth, erected in 1996, is what presides over this courtyard of baseball royalty. It presides — dominates — over the aluminum numbers. The statue, rising to a height of *sixteen feet*, is called Babe's Dream. It echoes back to the winsome days of a teenage phenom who honed his remarkable baseball skills at Baltimore's St. Mary's Industrial School under the tutelage of one Brother Matthias. Ruth, a native of Baltimore, never played a single game for the major-league Orioles in his life, but still merits a monumental statue on the very site reserved for all those Oriole greats.

There is also a statue of Ruth that was erected one year before then, in 1995, just outside the Sports Immortals Museum in Boca Raton, Florida.

In 2010 his rookie baseball card, for years on display at the Babe Ruth Museum, was quoted by *Forbes* as being worth a cool half million bucks and that card, only one of ten printed in 1914, is frayed at the ends.[9]

In 2013, another Ruth rookie card did sell and the price wasn't quite half a million, but close — $450,300. Yes, a Babe Ruth rookie card is a very good investment. In the second decade of the 21st century — when Babe Ruth is only the no. 3 man on the all-time home run list and the building where he played no longer stands and the number of people who actually saw him play dwindles with each passing day — Babe Ruth is worth more than ever.

There have been a number of biographies in print and two Hollywood films — the 1948 version called *The Babe Ruth Story* and in 1992 *The Babe*. A TV movie with Stephen Lang, which for Julia's money was better than Hollywood's two efforts, came out in 1991, but she says her favorite baseball film of all isn't one of those. She likes *The Sandlot*. It was a 1993 release about a group of boys who play on a rough-and-tumble sandlot only to lose a ball that had been signed by Babe Ruth when it gets slugged over the fence into a yard prowled by a monster dog. Actor James Earl Jones, who starred in the Kevin Costner film *Field of Dreams*, is in this one, too.

So what is it about Babe Ruth? There is the Babe Ruth League and the million-plus kids. The ridiculous prices attached to anything he touched. The pioneer and the humanitarian, and the iconic status that perhaps no other American has ever achieved, at least, not on so many fronts. We can start to gain a glimmer into understanding this phenomenon, into the mystique that he wears, by looking at Babe Ruth the man and some of the things he said. Like this gem:

If I just tried for them dinky singles I could've batted around .600.

For those not into baseball, a batting average of .600 — meaning that six times out of ten the batter gets a hit — is unheard of, and so is .500. The game hasn't seen a .400 hitter since Ted Williams got .406 in 1941, and the highest single-season batting average ever achieved by anyone was in 1894 when Hugh Duffy hit .440 for a team called the Boston Beaneaters. The closest any player has got to .400 since the end of World War II is Tony Gwynn of the San Diego Padres who in the 1994 season batted .394.

Brent Stevens, grandson of Julia and great-grandson of the Babe, has a website called www.BabeRuthCentral.com and one of the things he does is sell T-shirts with inspirational words from the man who coined them.

Never let the fear of striking out get in your way.
I swing big with everything I've got. I hit big and I miss big. I like to live as big as I can.
Every strike brings me closer to my next home run.
It's hard to beat a person who never gives up.

That last one is the biggest seller.

For $19.95 you can order a T-shirt with the quote on the front and image of a Babe Ruth-signed photo from the family's collection on the back. It's just one of the clothing lines from BRGoods. Stop and consider for a moment that these inspirational quotes are from a guy who never made it to high school. It adds to the luster. But another reason Babe Ruth will continue to grow is the character that he built for himself and the time and place he built it in — The Roaring Twenties and New York City. And it will continue because of the kind of person he was.

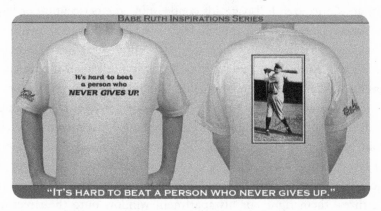

What kind of person was that? According to Julia, unwavering reliability was high on his list of attributes. She says that when he made a promise, he never broke it. There was the time he promised to attend her graduation from high school, but the day came and he was stuck in Albany, New York playing an exhibition game with the Yankees. So what did he do? He hired a plane and flew from Albany to Newark and that was a no-no. Baseball players were not allowed to fly in those days. It was considered too dangerous. Julia was sitting in the front row of the hall at her school with the other girls and all of a sudden this hush rose from the crowd. She turned around to see what the fuss was about, and there were Mother and *Daddy* walking through the door.

It didn't matter that the Yankees wouldn't allow their players to fly. Babe had made a promise to his daughter and would keep it come hell or high water. Another time Julia was in hospital with strep throat and needed a transfusion, so he told the doctors to test his blood and presto, they were a match. He gave her his blood and while the only real bloodlines between the two are from that transfusion, the bond was strong and remains strong to this day.

Another side to Babe Ruth was his sense of common decency and his pride in being American. In December, 1942, the World Jewish Congress organized full-page ads condemning the persecution of Jews by Nazi Germany. The ads appeared in major U.S. newspapers including *The New York Times*, and were signed by fifty prominent German-Americans. Ruth, who hailed from Pennsylvania Dutch immigrants, was the most famous name on the list. Then there was Pearl Harbor.

Julia was with her husband in New Hampshire, getting the lodge ready for the coming ski season, and obtained the precious details from her mother Claire. After the Japanese attacked Pearl Harbor on December 7, 1941, Babe was so infuriated that he threw out all the gifts he had received from his trip to Japan seven years earlier. He threw them right out his apartment window onto the street on Riverside Drive.

"He threw out everything except what Mother could catch," Julia recalls. "He was so furious about it."

Just how big was Babe Ruth? There is an old story about Japanese troops screaming 'To hell with Babe Ruth!' when they charged U.S. Marine lines during the war. This was even reported on page 2 in *The New York Times* on March 3, 1944. It was the most insulting thing the Japanese could say to the Americans they were fighting. What is so ironic is that the Japanese idolize Ruth themselves.

In the waning days of the war in the Pacific the brain trust of the United States actually considered having none other than Babe Ruth broadcast messages over the air waves to the Japanese. The Babe would ask them to lay down their arms and surrender. Maybe they would listen. It never happened, but what if it had? There would have been no atomic bombs dropped on Hiroshima or Nagasaki.

Babe Ruth would have changed history.

The life and times of Babe Ruth come with many highs and lows, both for him and baseball, and since he is the subject matter we can throw America into the mix, too.

As far as baseball is concerned, things were never lower than the infamous Black Sox scandal in the 1919 World Series when the heavily-favored Chicago White Sox lost to the upstart Cincinnati Reds by throwing the Series. They had taken a dive.

For the most part, salaries those days were low and several members of the White Sox stood to make more money by losing. It would cost them dearly as eight of their starting players would be kicked out of baseball for life. To this day, those suspensions are the biggest suspensions ever handed down by Major League Baseball. The one-season suspension served by Alex Rodriguez in 2014 is the biggest one since, but few people cried for A-Rod whose name and reputation were badly tarnished by the steroid scandal. Rodriguez is one of a long line of sluggers from recent history who may never gain entry into the National Baseball Hall of Fame because of using stimulants and because of the way they handled themselves when word got out. But back in 1919 the real hurt about the Black Sox scandal was what happened to the legendary Shoeless Joe Jackson.

Jackson was one of the game's greatest hitters and in 1919 was in the prime of his career. Ruth himself modeled his swing after Jackson's. But Jackson was a man who couldn't read or write, and despite the payoff to some players on his team, he would hit the only home run that his White Sox could muster in the entire series, not to mention lead the team in hits, runs and RBIs. His batting average for the World Series was .375 and that was even higher than anyone on the winning side. That statistic comes to light in the opening scene of the Kevin Costner film *Field of Dreams* when the erstwhile Iowa corn farmer tells his young daughter about the tragedy of Shoeless Joe Jackson.

Babe Ruth knew it was a tragedy, too, and he told Julia as much. Babe knew Jackson well and told Julia that the Chicago star had been in the dark about the whole thing from the get-go. Still, Jackson received the lifetime suspension and never played again. He died from a heart attack in 1951 at the age of sixty-four, and ever since the verdict came down he has been ruled ineligible for the Hall of Fame. According to Julia, 'Daddy' always said Jackson got a bum deal.

It was none other than Ruth himself who is credited with saving the integrity of the game. In 1919 he was no longer pitching full-time for the Boston Red Sox, but perched more often than not in right field. That year he set a new home-run record with twenty-nine. In 1920, one year after the scandal — the scandal that could have broken baseball — he was traded to the New York Yankees, and hit fifty-four homers his first season on Broadway and fifty-nine the next, breaking his own record each time out. The fans poured through the turnstiles. In 1923 they had to build a new stadium for him and in 1927 the Yankees with their Murderers' Row lineup were stocked knee-deep in stars. To this day that team is still regarded as the best in baseball history and that, of course, was the year he hit those sixty homers.

The legacy of Babe Ruth can't be measured in the way one measures personal accomplishments in baseball or other sports or even other lines of work for that matter. After all, a legacy is not a number. But a legacy does have magnitude and what is increasingly rare these days, staying power. On these two fronts Babe Ruth is unique.

Many icons turn out to be bigger in death than they ever were in life, often due to the circumstances of their demise. We have the assassinations of presidents and public figures, and the tragic deaths of movie stars and other celebrities who were taken before their time. Babe Ruth was taken before his time, too. He was only fifty-three. But he is different than a John F. Kennedy, an Abraham Lincoln, a Martin Luther King, or for that matter an Elvis Presley or a Marilyn Monroe. He is different because, even after all this time, his star continues to rise.

In 1995, the Hofstra Cultural Centre at Hofstra University in Hempstead, New York held a conference called *Baseball and the Sultan of Swat* to commemorate the centennial of Ruth's birth. On the first morning of the conference, the program brochure was handed out to all the attendees with a message from Eric J. Schmertz, the Hofstra law professor who was serving as director of the gathering. In the message this is what he said:

> "We will spend these three days in April talking and thinking about Babe Ruth, a man of history. That we do so 100 years after his birth, 80 years after his first major league game, 75 years after he was sold by the Boston Red Sox to the New York Yankees, 68 years after he hit 60 home runs, 60 years after his last game, and 47 years after his death is compelling evidence of the immense magnitude of his legacy."

Schmertz went on to pose a question. Why would a university, an institution of scholarship and higher learning no less, devote such time, resources and energy to a sports figure? His response:

> "Our answer is that Babe Ruth was more than a sports figure. He remains a major presence with continuing influence on subjects intellectual, educational, and cultural, well removed from the baseball diamond."

That conference got into everything there was to get into about Ruth. Literature. Poetry. Art. Ethics. International affairs. Politics. Film. Law. Advertising. Music. Vaudeville. Psychology. And legend. There were scholars, biographers, historians, sports and baseball people, even a physicist who presented a paper examining the intricate dynamics of his swing.

Everything went according to schedule except that then New York City Mayor Rudy Giuliani, who was supposed to deliver a keynote address, failed to show. Someone else who didn't show was former slugger and Hall of Famer Ralph Kiner. But Kiner, who passed away in 2014, wasn't supposed to attend. Not in person anyway. Kiner — after his playing days he became the play-by-play announcer for the New York Mets — appeared via video on a big screen and in the interview he was asked how many home runs he thought Babe Ruth would hit if he was playing in the present day. The place went silent.

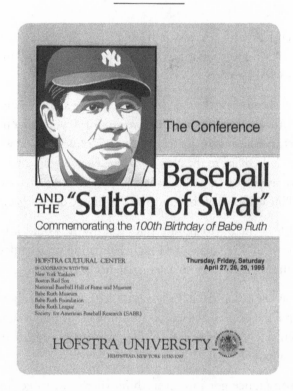

The Conference

Baseball
AND THE "Sultan of Swat"

Commemorating the *100th Birthday of Babe Ruth*

HOFSTRA CULTURAL CENTER
IN COOPERATION WITH THE
New York Yankees
Boston Red Sox
National Baseball Hall of Fame and Museum
Babe Ruth Museum
Babe Ruth Foundation
Babe Ruth League
Society for American Baseball Research (SABR)

Thursday, Friday, Saturday
April 27, 28, 29, 1995

HOFSTRA UNIVERSITY
HEMPSTEAD, NEW YORK 11550-1090

"About twenty," he said.

"Twenty? Is that all?" the questioner asked.

"Yes," said Kiner. "But you have to understand. He would be a hundred years old."

Of all the special guests on hand at that conference, the one who received the biggest ovation was Mel Allen, long-time announcer of the New York Yankees. Allen, who would pass away the following year, made note of the fact that it was forty-eight years earlier — to the very day — when Ruth had appeared at Yankee Stadium on Babe Ruth Day. That was to be his last appearance in a baseball uniform. At the conference Allen repeated the Babe's speech from that memorable afternoon, which had been a poignant moment for the tens of thousands of Ruth admirers who knew that the great Bambino was in ill health.

On the first morning of the conference at Hofstra there were personal greetings from the Babe Ruth Family — Julia Ruth Stevens and her son Tom Stevens. Tom spoke and in his remarks he told the attendees about some of Julia's more poignant recollections of her father. In the afternoon the Honourable Kurt L. Schmoke, who was Mayor of Baltimore when the conference was held in 1995, represented the city of Ruth's birth. He talked about the sixteen-foot statue of Ruth that would soon be unveiled at Camden Yards, home of the Baltimore Orioles. The statue was called Babe's Dream. But sixteen feet?

"Babe Ruth dreamed big," Schmoke said.

"The world of sports has lost one of its greatest figures and his kids have lost their greatest idol."
— Tris Speaker

Chapter 3

THE LEGACY BEGINS

As baseball banners fly at half-mast . . . and silent fans stand with bowed heads . . . we join the rest of the Baseball world in solemn tribute to the memory of Babe Ruth.

Our association with the Babe, since the beginning of his long and glorious career, developed between him and many members of our concern close, personal friendships that have endured through the years.

No player has contributed more to the Game . . . none has furnished more thrills for the fans . . . none is more deserving of the number one spot in the heart of Baseball.

HILLERICH & BRADSBY COMPANY

BABE RUTH DIED on August 16, 1948. He was fifty-three years old and the cause of death was cancer. According to news reports immediately after his death, a malignant tumor on the left side of his neck had been partially removed the previous year, but doctors were unable to get it all. A new drug had been tried which initially seemed to work since the mass in his neck had apparently disappeared and his pain had dissipated. The drug — teropterin — had been tried previously in mice. In fact, Ruth's condition had improved so much after taking the drug that the case was even reported at an International Cancer Congress in St. Louis in September, 1947 with the name of the famous subject carefully concealed. But the effects would prove to be temporary.

A few weeks before he died he had been administered the last rites of the Catholic Church, but managed to rally and get back on his feet to make one final public appearance. That was to attend the premier of the movie *The Babe Ruth Story*. He then returned to Memorial Hospital in New York City and never left.

It was no secret that he had been in ill health, but the word *cancer* had been avoided. More than a year earlier — on Sunday, April 27, 1947 — it was Babe Ruth Day at all major league parks in baseball. On that day he appeared in the flesh at Yankee Stadium, gaunt, just a shadow of his former self, with 60,000 people turning out to honor him.

The day after his death *The New York Times* ran the lead story under the headline 'Babe Ruth, Baseball Idol, Dies at 53 After Lingering Illness.' It ran in the middle of the front page with a large photograph, and inside was a full-page story and more photos still. The headline inside called him 'Baseball's Great Star and Idol of Children.'

The obituary by *Times* reporter Murray Schumach began this way:

'Probably nowhere in all the imaginative field of fiction could one find a career more dramatic and bizarre than that portrayed in real life by George Herman Ruth. Known the world over, even in foreign lands where baseball is never played, as the Babe, he was the boy who rose from the obscurity of a charitable institution in Baltimore to a position as the leading figure in professional baseball. He was also its greatest drawing-card, its highest salaried performer — at least of his day — and the idol of millions of youngsters throughout the land.'[10]

Schumach went on to describe how Ruth had appeared in his final days.

'The powerful six-footer who had once electrified Americans with sixty homers in a season had wasted away. The famous round face had become so hollowed that his snub nose looked long. The once black hair so often seen when the Babe doffed his cap rounding the bases was almost white.'

Another story in *The Times* that day said Ruth never knew about his cancer malady. Yet another told how more than 31,000 fans rose for a moment of silence in Boston at a National League game between the Dodgers and Braves, and another still said how Ruth was now the seventh member of the 1927 Yankees team to pass away. Running with those articles was a list — 'Ruth's Pay by Seasons During Baseball Career.' It began with the $600 salary he had earned in 1914 as a member of the International League Baltimore Orioles, reaching a high of $80,000 a year with the Yankees in the 1930 and 1931 seasons, and finishing with a salary of $40,000 with the National League Boston Braves in 1935. There was also the $15,000 he had earned in 1938 as a member of the Brooklyn Dodgers (first-base coach), for a grand total of $925,000 in total earnings for his career. It was a monumental sum for the time — especially for a baseball player.

The night before his death more than 15,000 messages were received at the hospital and they came from all across North America. His wife Claire personally received hundreds of telegrams through Western Union after his passing.

Branch Rickey, president of the Brooklyn Baseball Club and the man who is best known for bringing Jackie Robinson into the major leagues, said this in a telegram sent to Mrs. George H. Ruth at Yankee Stadium:

> 'It must give you much satisfaction and comfort to know that his spirit lives on in the hearts and minds of sports-loving Americans of all ages as a continuing inspiration to youth and a fond memory to those of an earlier generation.'[11]

Louis R. Perini, President of the Boston Braves, said in his telegram:

> 'The entire personnel of the Boston Braves family joins baseball people everywhere in paying tribute to the memory of your husband whose contributions to our national game will live long after all of us have seen our final contest. On this day dedicated to the Babe, it is our prayer that the youngsters of today and tomorrow may always look upon him as one whose success in his life's work must by all odds be considered one of the great tributes to the privilege of living in a democracy.'[12]

The telegram from a man named Walter Trumbull said:

> 'The Babe was infinitely more than a great athlete. He was a shining symbol of courage under pressure and kindness in adversity and men admired and respected him. But kids loved him and that may be the finer epitaph.'[13]

This came from William M. Tuck, Governor of Virginia:

> 'The people of Virginia extend their deepest sympathy in the loss of your distinguished husband whose contributions to character building and good sportsmanship were universally admired.'[14]

From baseball great Tris Speaker:

'The world of sports has lost one of its greatest figures and his kids have lost their greatest idol.'[15]

And from Arch Ward, sports editor of *The Chicago Tribune*:

'I hope you will get some comfort out of the realization that for many years you had the privilege of living with the most popular man American sport has produced.'[16]

Murray Schumach, the man who wrote the obit in *The New York Times*, may have understood Ruth better than most. A native of Brooklyn, Schumach was a college dropout who had learned his craft as a police reporter working nights. When he died in 2004 at the age of ninety-one — his career with the newspaper spanned some forty-eight years — his own obit carried this comment from Arthur Gelb, his former managing editor.

"Murray grew up in the Depression years and he understood the poor and could convey that beautifully to readers."[17]

In short, Schumach *knew* Babe Ruth. After Ruth's death he wrote:

'The range of greetings to the ailing man, who was more famous in his heyday than Presidents, showed how strong a hold he still had on the people.'

Newspaper accounts in America and around the world provided more than a glimmer of the public's fascination with him. This, again, from Schumach:

'A creation of the times, he seemed to embody all the qualities that a sport-loving nation demanded of its outstanding hero. For it has always been debatable whether Ruth owed his fame and the vast fortune it made for him more to his ability to smash home runs in greater quantity than any other player in the history of the game or to a strange personality that at all times was intensely real and "regular," which was the one fixed code by which he lived.

'He made friends by the thousands and rarely, if ever, lost any of them. Affable, boisterous and good-natured to a fault, he was always as accessible to the newsboy on the corner as to the most dignified personage in worldly affairs. More, he could be very much at ease with both.'[18]

In *The New York Times* that day was a photo of Ruth with actor Gary Cooper that had been taken during the filming of the movie *Pride of the Yankees* which was about the life of Lou Gehrig. There was another photo showing the powerful young pitcher of the Boston Red Sox in the year of his major-league debut — 1914 — and directly below that a shot of a very ill Ruth in his last days. And there was also a photo of him coaching young students on a visit to France in 1935.

Babe Ruth was a universal figure. A few days after he died a United States ocean liner called *America* pulled into port in New York City — from Europe — and the passengers contributed $3,784 for a cancer fund in his memory.

He was known everywhere and to everyone. Plastered across the front page of *The Baltimore News-Post* were the words 'BABE RUTH DIES AT 53.' *The New York Daily Mirror* had but four words — 'BABE RUTH IS DEAD' — as did *The San Francisco Examiner* — 'DEATH TAKES BABE RUTH.' *The New York Daily News* had only three — 'BABE RUTH DIES' and so did *The Sporting News* — 'NATION MOURNS RUTH.'

The headline for *The Christian Science Monitor* was 'Tributes to Babe Ruth Pour In From All Walks of Life' and even in the United Kingdom *The Derby Daily Telegraph* ran this headline — 'Babe Ruth Dies' — followed by the sub-headline 'U.S. Tributes To Baseball Immortal.'

But in the days following his death it was *The New York Times* that delivered the most ink and explored in depth the enormous impact he had on the nation. An article called 'Last Out for the Babe' by Arthur Daley said this:

'It had to come sometime, of course. But Babe Ruth seemingly had acquired a look of immortality as if he were a demi-god who had sprung from Zeus. He was not an ordinary mortal even in life. Now in death he will assume still more grandiose proportions as an almost legendary figure. The Babe was a truly fabulous man, the best beloved and the best known person of our times, greater even than the sport which spawned him.'[19]

Later in that same article Daley wrote:

'The hold that Ruth had on the public never has been matched by anyone in sport or out of it. He commanded it by just being himself, the most natural and unaffected man in this wide world.'[20]

Ruth would lie in state in the rotunda at Yankee Stadium for two solid days. On August 17th an endless stream of mourners estimated at 50,000 people would file past his open casket. The next day, August 18th, the number of mourners was said to be even higher — 55,000. Nobody knows for sure how many people came over those two days, but some estimates go as high as 200,000. The funeral was held the day after that at St. Patrick's Cathedral with Cardinal Francis Spellman, the sixth Archbishop of New York, conducting the service; 6,000 people were on hand while another 75,000 stood outside in the pouring rain.

It has been said that Babe Ruth's funeral was the biggest one ever held in the United States for a person who wasn't in the military and who wasn't in politics. In other words, it was the biggest funeral ever for a private American citizen. Cardinal Spellman, presiding at the requiem mass, spoke the final prayer:

'May the Divine Spirit that inspired Babe Ruth to overcome hardships and win the crucial game of life animate many generations of American youth to learn from the examples of his struggles and successes loyally to play their positions on all American teams. May his generous-hearted soul, through the mercy of God, the final scoring of his own good deeds, and the prayers of his faithful friends, rest in everlasting peace.'

After the service came the funeral procession and, as with everything else about the Babe, it was larger than life. The procession began in Manhattan and required 250 police officers to direct the motorcade which filed past Yankee Stadium before winding its way out of the city to Westchester and then the hamlet of Hawthorne. And once again thousands upon thousands — the crowd was estimated at over 100,000 people — lined the route. At the cemetery more thousands still were waiting for him.

The pallbearers were the legendary ballplayer, manager and team owner Connie Mack, sportswriter Fred Lieb, and two former Yankee teammates of Ruth's — Joe Dugan and Waite Hoyt. There was also a long list of honorary pallbearers. They included the governor of New York State and the mayors of New York City, Boston and Baltimore, not to mention the senior brass from the world of baseball, Yankees star outfielder Joe DiMaggio, former world heavyweight boxing champion Jack Dempsey, and actor William Bendix who had portrayed the Babe in *The Babe Ruth Story*.

At the National Baseball Hall of Fame and Museum in Cooperstown, New York, the first words on Ruth's plaque are: *'Biggest drawing card in history of baseball.'* He certainly was — and is — the biggest draw in both life and death.

How big? Mike Barnicle, writing more than fifty years later in the September 14, 1999 issue of *ESPN The Magazine*, said this about Ruth:

"He was the biggest thing in the world. He was the loudest noise in a land made mute by poverty and unemployment. Long before Palmer or Jordan, Woods or Ali, Babe Ruth smothered America with his presence. And he did it at a time where there was no television, computers, cell phones, Internet, coffee bars or ESPN. He was a walking, talking highlight film each and every day of his life, both on and off the field, most of it created and nurtured through word of mouth, a mountain of newspaper stories and the fact that he was the most marvelous ballplayer of all time."[21]

In 1998 ESPN produced a documentary called *Outside the Lines: Babe Ruth's Larger Than Life Legacy.* One of the people interviewed was noted newspaper columnist George F. Will who said:

"Ruth was the first national superstar — the man who gave us that category."[22]

Will made that observation half a century after Ruth died. But why was he *the first national superstar?* Some of the sentiments expressed immediately following his death may help to explain it. Baseball writer H. G. Salinger of *The Detroit News* wrote this shortly after his passing:

"What attracted so many people to Ruth? He was rowdy, rough, tough, profane, ribald, swaggering. He had most of the human faults and weaknesses, but he also had most of the human virtues and probably the greatest of them were honesty, complete unselfishness, charity and love for his fellow man. Ruth never pretended to be anything but what he was."[23]

It may have been Harry Hooper, a one-time teammate of Ruth's on the Boston Red Sox, who said it best:

"Sometimes I still can't believe what I saw. This 19-year-old kid, crude, poorly educated, only lightly brushed by the social veneer we call civilization, gradually transformed into the idol of American youth and the symbol of baseball the world over — a man loved by more people and with an intensity of feeling that perhaps has never been equaled before or since."[24]

Sportswriter Chris Dufresne of *The Los Angeles Times* wrote a feature about Ruth that was published on July 12, 2014 to commemorate the 100th anniversary of the Babe's first appearance in the major leagues. That appearance had taken place on July 11, 1914 when he first appeared as a pitcher for the Boston Red Sox at Fenway Park.

The piece was called '*100 years after big league debut, Babe Ruth is still larger than life.*' As to why Ruth still mattered a whole century later, Dufresne may have hit it home with this candid observation:

"Ruth endures because enough truth exists between the lies."

A few days after he died the Hillerich & Bradsby Company — makers of the Louisville Slugger bat that he had used to such acclaim — took out a full-page ad in *The New York Times*. The ad depicted a huge drawing of Ruth's familiar round face next to a flagpole with a pennant that just said *BASEBALL*. And there were these words:

'As baseball banners fly at half mast ... and silent fans stand with bowed heads ... we join the rest of the Baseball world in solemn tribute to the memory of Babe Ruth. Our association with the Babe, since the beginning of his long and glorious career, developed between him and many members of our concern close personal friendships that have endured through the years. No player has contributed more to the Game ... none has furnished more thrills for the fans ... none is more deserving of the number one spot in the heart of Baseball.'

The year before he died Ruth had established the Babe Ruth Foundation Inc., which was dedicated to the interests of underprivileged children. He even made the first contribution himself and after his passing his estate would give ten per cent of its annual income to the fund. Charities were a big part — a major part — of his life, as was anything to do with kids.

There was also a light side, a comical side, to Ruth that played no small part in making him what he was, and when coupled with those legions of young fans, it made for an irresistible combination. The 1928 silent film *Speedy* by Harold Lloyd is a good example.

Lloyd, a huge star in the silent era, starred and produced the film which is essentially a wild ride through the streets of New York City. *Speedy* is about a taxi driver who, the Keystone Kops aside, may have

given birth to the classic movie chase except no one is really being chased in this scene. The film begins with taxi driver Lloyd spotting Ruth outside an orphanage. Ruth, looking trim and dapper in a suit, is being mobbed by scores of kids as he tosses them one signed baseball after another. Then he summons the taxi and tells the driver that he has to get to Yankee Stadium.

Fast.

Lloyd obliges and drives like a crazy man as he dotes on his illustrious passenger in the back seat, constantly looking over his shoulder to talk to the Babe, not paying attention to the road. At first Ruth is calm and cool, but as the car goes through one near miss after another he becomes more and more agitated. Finally, they arrive at Yankee Stadium with Ruth's classic send-off line: "If I ever want to commit suicide I'll call you."

It's only a silent movie with no spoken words, but Ruth is funny and genuine — a natural — so unlike many sports figures who become comatose robots when in front of a camera. *Speedy*, which was Lloyd's last short silent film, was even nominated for an Oscar that year in the category Best Director of a Comedy.

Sportswriter Roger Kahn, probably best known for his baseball book *The Boys of Summer* (Harper & Row, 1972), did a piece on Babe Ruth in the August 1959 edition of *Esquire*. Much of the article, written eleven years after Ruth's death, got into the seedier side of his life, but even here there was popular spectacle at play. In the article Kahn mentions an incident that allegedly took place in 1924 when a prominent family in Delaware was holding a party and they wanted a few of the Yankees to attend. And they wanted Ruth. He turned out to be the life of the party, but the team had a game with Philadelphia the next day and had to hit the road. According to Kahn's article, the Babe had met some young lady at the party and didn't want to leave. However, a boxing promoter who was there said he could take care of that sort of thing for him in Philly.

When the game began at Shibe Park in Philadelphia the next afternoon, Ruth announced that he was feeling good. But another player, a teammate, told him he didn't look that well, so the Babe bet him $100 that he would hit a home run in the game. The player replied that Shibe Park was an easy place to hit a home run, so Ruth then offered him odds of two-to-one.

They made the bet.

Wrote Kahn in the *Esquire* article: 'On his first time at-bat, Ruth walloped an outside pitch into the left-field stands and won his bet. Then he lined a triple to right, crashed a triple over Al Simmons' head in center and pulled a homer over the right-field wall. He had gone four for four, with two triples and two homers, without benefit of bed rest.'

It all goes into the mix that was Babe Ruth.

"He's larger than life, and as we move further away from his playing days every year, his legacy doesn't shrink. It grows because of the lasting impact he had on the game."
— *Jeff Idelson, President,*
National Baseball Hall of Fame and Museum

Chapter 4

———

THE FACE OF COOPERSTOWN

IN THE EARLY DAYS of professional baseball Albert G. Spalding was a star pitcher who throughout his career would rack up an impressive 262 wins against only 65 losses. He was born in 1850 and began his career in 1871 with the Boston Red Stockings, a team that played in the very first professional league — the National Association. Spalding, the perennial leader in wins, hung up his uniform in 1878 with the Chicago White Stockings. By that time the league was called the National League. After his playing days were over, Spalding became a team owner and a supplier to baseball; he and his brother founded the A. G. Spalding sports goods company in 1876 and it is still around today. In addition, he published baseball guides and instruction manuals. He died in 1915.

Spalding was a very influential figure from the early years of baseball. Another influential figure of the time was Henry Chadwick who was born in England in 1824.

Chadwick's family came to the United States when he was thirteen and by the mid-1850s he was a cricket writer for *The New York Times*. He was soon hired by another newspaper to write about a newer sport that was rapidly gaining in popularity. Baseball. Chadwick became well known as a baseball historian and statistician, and helped created the notion of box scores, the batting average, and the pitcher's earned run average (ERA). In 1861, in the early days of the Civil War, he organized a baseball game between the Brooklyn nine and the New York nine. At the time it was considered to be a healthy respite from the public stress of war engulfing the nation. Chadwick eventually became the editor for Albert Spalding's *Official Baseball Guide* which came out every year. He died in 1908.

Both these men were posthumously elected to the National Baseball Hall of Fame.

The two were friends, but back in 1905 their paths would cross over a dispute about the origins of baseball. Spalding, ever the patriot, claimed that the game had been invented by an American in the United States, while Chadwick had a different view. He said baseball had evolved from the old English game of rounders which involved a bat and a ball. In fact, there are records going back to the 18th century and a book published in 1744 does mention the hyphenated word *base-ball*.[25]

Nevertheless, Spalding appointed a commission to study the matter and in 1908 it concluded that one Abner Doubleday had invented the game in Cooperstown, New York — and not only that — it had happened in 1839. Consider this to be baseball's creation story. Doubleday was a prominent Union general in the Civil War who had fought at Gettsyburg. He died in 1893 and there was no mention in his diaries about baseball or anything to do with baseball. Nothing. The tale turned out to be just that — a fanciful tale — but because of the myth the National Baseball Hall of Fame and Museum would find its home in Cooperstown, a small town that built, and continues to enjoy, a tourism-based economy complete with the 'historic' Doubleday Field, the so-called birthplace of baseball.

For what it's worth, in 2011 Major League Baseball established a panel of experts and historians — the Baseball Origins Committee — to solve the conundrum once and for all, and when last heard they were still working on it. However, the Doubleday story has been shown to be pure fiction, never mind that over the years more than one President has bought into the story and made public reference to it, not the least of whom was Franklin D. Roosevelt.[26]

The saga of Abner Doubleday doing his momentous thing at Cooperstown is just one of many myths perpetuated about American history. There are many, of course, such as the celebrated romance between Pocahontas and John Smith which has often been captured in song and film. Only it never happened. Another one is Paul Revere's cry 'The British are coming! The British are coming!' during his famous ride warning the locals in the War of Independence. It didn't exactly happen like that either. How about George Washington cutting down the cherry tree? That is bogus as well. Never mind what really took place at such portentous events as the 1881 shootout at the O.K. Corral or the Alamo in 1836.

Hollywood hasn't helped, and neither has it helped where Babe Ruth is concerned. But there is a world of difference between those other stories and all matters *Ruthian*.

Imagine a wide receiver in football who forges record after record with his amazing catches and then they see how far and how accurately he can *throw* the ball. So he changes positions and becomes the greatest quarterback in football history.

Nothing like this has ever transpired.

Imagine a goaltender in hockey who sets a new standard in puck stopping only to emerge later as the game's greatest ever *goal scorer*.

Nope.

How about a simple-minded young lad without much of an upbringing who is sent to a boys' school where an Xaverian Brother, a giant of a man no less, teaches him the fine art of baseball? The kid is so good the pros come calling and they sign him as a pitcher, and what a pitcher he gets to be — the best lefthander in the American League who would toss twenty-nine consecutive scoreless innings in the World Series, a record that would stand for some forty-two years. Then that same kid turns out to be the greatest slugger of all-time! Such is the reality of Babe Ruth which brings us to Cooperstown and the National Baseball Hall of Fame and Museum.

On February 2, 1936, the first five members of the Baseball Hall of Fame were announced to the world. The five charter members, in order of the number of votes cast for them, were: Ty Cobb with 222, Babe Ruth with 215, Honus Wagner with 215, Christy Mathewson with 205, and Walter Johnson with 189. This means that of the 226 sports writers who at the time belonged to the Baseball Writers Association of America, eleven of them did *not* vote for Babe Ruth. One can only wonder what they were drinking, and keep in mind this was all of one year after Ruth had retired. If it's any consolation, at no time in the history of the sport has there ever been a unanimous selection to the Hall of Fame.

Still, these players were the first five inductees. Three years later on June 12, 1939, four of those charter members — Christy Mathewson had died in 1925 — were on hand at the first induction ceremony in Cooperstown, and were joined by other players who had been named between 1937 and 1939.

Ruth took his spot in a now legendary photograph that was notable for the absence of Ty Cobb; Cobb had arrived at the ceremony late after the iconic picture had already been taken. Standing in the back row of that shot from the 1939 induction ceremony were: Honus Wagner, Grover Cleveland Alexander, Tris Speaker, Nap Lajoie, George Sisler, and Walter Johnson. Seated in front of them were: Eddie Collins, Babe Ruth, Connie Mack, and Cy Young. Nine of those ten men were clad in jacket and tie. Only Ruth was without a tie, but he did have the jacket.

In his book *Induction Day at Cooperstown* (McFarland & Company, Inc., Jefferson, North Carolina and London, 2011), author Dennis Corcoran describes the events of that memorable day:

> 'A huge crowd gathered, jamming Main Street all the way to the traffic light on Pioneer Street. Many fans perched on parked cars, leaned out windows, or found other vantage points, such as rooftops, in order to see the proceedings.'[27]

Corcoran, who actually managed to interview people who had been at that 1939 ceremony, writes how a band played *Take Me out to the Ballgame* before Connie Mack, seventy-six at the time and still manager of the Philadelphia Athletics, thanked the people of Cooperstown for "having the game of baseball start here."[28]

Ten of those early inductees were allowed to say a few words, and back then the words were few indeed, not like Hall of Fame inductions today. Ruth was the last to speak and his words have been captured on film.

So, how much does he mean to Cooperstown? For starters, there is no mistaking his huge presence in the town itself. Even today. He is everywhere. In the storefront of a shop on Main Street a row of sweaters hangs in the window with the players' names on the back — Strawberry, Fisk, Yount, Yastrzemski, Gwynn, Ripken, Clemens, Ruth. His is the only one from the old days. In another shop, right beside a sign promoting Abbott and Costello's *'Who's on First?'* routine on DVD, is a photo of Ruth walking with bat in hand and one of his quotes — "Yesterday's home runs don't win today's games." Everywhere one goes on Main Street it is more of the same, and at the Hall of Fame and Museum the Ruth presence is even more prominent.

Inside the building, up on a screen in the main lobby, a series of images appears as a slide show. One image acknowledges the current World Series champions. Another highlights the next round of Hall of Fame inductees. The third is about an app that lets you 'Create your own Hall of Fame baseball cards' on an iPhone. And the fourth, with a photo of Babe Ruth, is about the Hall of Fame's Digital Preservation Project.

In the ever-bustling Museum Store the cashiers do a brisk business and on the wall directly behind them is a photo of Babe Ruth and Lou Gehrig from their Yankee heydays. In the gift shop is a reproduction of the front page of *The Los Angeles Evening Herald* from September 30, 1927 and the headline: *'RUTH HITS 60TH HOME RUN.'*

At the end of the long hall where the revered player plaques are on display — if the Hall of Fame has a holy place, this is it — there are two statues of hitters. They are life-size and remarkably life-like. Visitors always take photographs posing with this pair of sluggers. One of them is a rightie for the Boston Red Sox — Ted Williams — and the other is a leftie for the New York Yankees.

Ruth.

The sculptor who made them, Armand LaMontagne, carved each statue from a single piece of basswood and the effect is amazing. The Ruth statue, unveiled in 1984, immediately became a huge attraction at the Hall of Fame and was prominently positioned in the main lobby. The next year 'Ruth' was joined by the statue of Williams and then both of them were moved to that long hall with the plaques.

On the main floor of the Hall of Fame is a gallery called *Art of Baseball* and the first thing one sees is this massive face on canvas. Wide nose, Yankees cap, and eyes that can only be called intense. The huge portrait is right beside the name of the gallery and the face looks like it is staring back at you. Walk inside the gallery and up on the wall is a big painting of Ruth at the plate pointing to the outfield — his Called Shot Home Run — in a scene that appears almost biblical.

The most popular part of the Hall of Fame is on the second floor. Up the stairs and to the left are the LOCKER ROOM and GRANDSTAND THEATER. To the right are galleries reserved for the respective eras of the game and special categories: TAKING THE FIELD (19th century), THE GAME (20th century), PRIDE AND PASSION (old Negro Leagues and pre-Negro Leagues), DIAMOND DREAMS (women in baseball), ¡VAVA BASEBALL (Latin American players), WHOLE NEW BALLGAME (starting with the 1970s), and BABE RUTH (life and legend).

The Sultan of Swat merits his own section.

Henry Aaron has an exhibit, too. They are the only two players with their very own galleries, but one doesn't feel the presence of Aaron, or any other player for that matter, the way one feels, or absorbs, the presence of Ruth. It is omnipotent and seems to exude from every nook and cranny. He is

on the cover of the Hall of Fame brochure guide, or at least, his things are on the cover. In fact, *only* Babe Ruth items are on the cover of the guide — his glove, a signed baseball, his cleats, his no. 3 sweater, a signed bat.

In 2014 the Ruth exhibit received a makeover. It reopened on July 14 that year and the date was significant because it marked the 100th anniversary of his major-league debut with the Red Sox. Wrote Craig Muder, who at the time was the Hall's Director of Communications: "Ruth's legend was more than just numbers. He became an oversized symbol of America's power, a brilliant man with human flaws that made him seem more real than mythic."

If there ever was a character where myth and reality are intertwined — and it can be hard to hard to tell where one ends and the other begins — it is Ruth.

The Babe Ruth exhibit occupies less than 200 square feet, but not an inch of space is wasted. It begins with a statement up on the wall:

> "From Babe Ruth's meteoric rise as a dominant southpaw to his endless barrage of tape-measure home runs to his larger-than-life personality, the press of the day chronicled his every move both on and off the field. Turn back the pages of time and revisit Babe's life and legend … as it happened."

The first thing in the exhibit is the Yankee jersey Ruth wore on June 13, 1948 when his number was officially retired. It is the same jersey from the Nat Fein photo that would win the Pulitzer Prize, and the blown-up photo is right there alongside it, making for an eerie effect. Ruth also wore this jersey in his cameo appearance playing himself in the 1942 film *Pride of the Yankees* which starred Gary Cooper as Lou Gehrig. And he wore it in benefit games, like the time he batted against Walter Johnson when they were both retired and busy raising money for war bonds.

The first wall of the exhibit depicts his 'Troubled youth in Baltimore' and then moves on to his playing for the minor-league

Orioles and his subsequent introduction to the big leagues. Displayed here is a reproduction of the transfer agreement that sent Ruth and two other players from those same Baltimore Orioles to the Boston Red Sox on July 9, 1914. There are newspaper clippings and photos galore, not to mention an audio constantly playing his speech from the 1947 appearance at Babe Ruth Day at Yankee Stadium. There is also an audio of him relating, in his own words, his Called Shot Home Run from the 1932 World Series, and old newsreels of things that he did — such as visiting hospitals.

He did a lot of that.

The exhibit moves on through the other phases of his life in baseball and afterward in chronological fashion, and that is precisely the point.

Tom Shieber, senior curator at the Hall of Fame, was lead curator for the exhibit and is no stranger to Babe Ruth. He has worked at the Hall since 1998. Shieber said the exhibit was due for a revamping and the idea was to reveal Ruth's story in a compelling manner. He makes no bones about the fact that the very purpose of the Hall of Fame is to tell stories of interest to the public.

"A seven-year-old who comes to the Hall knows who Babe Ruth is," Shieber says. "When you think about that it is remarkable. Ruth is a legend now and he was a legend in his own time. With the exhibit our task was to understand the phenomenon that was Babe Ruth and you can only do that in one of two ways. You can get into a time machine, but we're a non-profit and can't afford that. Or you can create a scrapbook, which is a virtual time machine, and that's what we did."

Says Shieber: "I was really an editor. Most of what you read in the exhibit are articles penned by reporters and headlines written by headline writers. It was a massive research project and I came away with a greater appreciation for how popular Ruth was at the time, especially in his early career. He was a dominant force in baseball even before he came to the Yankees. There were newspaper reporters whose only job was to cover Babe Ruth! That's all they did. It's the fact that Ruth's impact goes so far beyond baseball that makes him truly exceptional."

Shieber says there are other personalities who might be close, in terms of a *craze*, in terms of a *phenomenon*, and he singles out Frank Sinatra and The Beatles. He says it would only apply to Sinatra when he was at his absolute peak, but then Ol' Blue Eyes didn't have the charisma of Babe Ruth. As for The Beatles, with them it was shared among four while with Ruth it was just the one.

"He was larger than life and he goes beyond home runs," says Shieber. "Things today are referred to as *Ruthian*. In one section of the exhibit we see how Ruth's name became synonymous with greatness. Newspapers exclaimed that Pele was the Babe Ruth of soccer and Gene Krupa was the Babe Ruth of drummers."

Indeed, the exhibit has a clipping of hockey star Gordie Howe that refers to him as *'The Babe Ruth of hockey.'*

Shieber says when visitors come through the doors of the Hall of Fame somewhere in their brain they have to be thinking about Ruth.

"People would be shocked if we didn't have a Babe Ruth exhibit. Why does the typical seven-year-old know who he is? That's the

$64,000 question. I just don't really understand it myself but all I can tell you is it happens."

The exhibit aside, another area in the Hall of Fame — the Giamatti Research Center — is the place where everything you want to know about Babe Ruth but are afraid to ask exists in abundance. This is the library of the National Baseball Hall of Fame and Museum, and it is the biggest and most foremost repository of baseball information anywhere in the entire world. The repository is now digital (i.e., Digital Preservation Project). The total collection includes *three million items* and we are talking books, periodicals, archival manuscripts and photographs, audiovisual materials, team publications, databases, and scrapbooks.

The scrapbooks come in six distinct groupings. One scrapbook was given to the Hall of Fame from the family of Andrew Rube Foster, a prominent pitcher in the old Negro Leagues who later became a manager and who lived from 1879 to 1930. Another one is for Art Pennington, a later player from the Negro Leagues who also toiled for teams in Cuba and Mexico before he made it to minor-league pro teams in the United States. That one covers the 1940s and 1950s. The Big Bill Smith scrapbook is for yet another veteran from the old Negro Leagues and covers the early 1900s.

The Jackie Robinson scrapbook explores the period from 1947 to 1956 and focuses on the man who broke major-league baseball's color bar. Yet another scrapbook centers on the 1971 season of a fundraising, fastball team from Quebec called Les 4 Chevaliers.

Then we have Babe Ruth.

If there is any doubt that he was the most followed and chronicled person of his day, a visit to the Giamatti Research Center provides ample evidence. The whole collection has been digitized which is a good thing because there are volumes upon volumes of scrapbooks, divided and sub-divided into various sections. If looking for items from his life (1895-1948), one can choose from twenty-five different scrapbooks. That's right. *Twenty-five.* There are scrapbooks under the heading of Christy Walsh, who was Ruth's agent, and others still under such headings as Home Runs, New York Yankees, World Series, Sports Contracts, Vaudeville, Barnstorming, Miller Huggins who was the manager of those great Yankee teams, and even Mrs. Babe Ruth.

The Babe Ruth scrapbooks are a library of the life and times of Babe Ruth. They are the legacy of that same Christy Walsh who first put them together — twenty-five volumes filling some 1,400 pages — and what immediately hits you when going through them is how everything Ruth did seemed to be reported in the press.

'RUTH HEADS FOR SAN DIEGO' reads a mammoth headline from the San Diego *Evening Tribune* (October 28, 1924).

'*Six Heroes Greet Their Idol ... And Bam Shows 'Em How it's Done*' screams another headline from the *New York Evening Journal* (May 20, 1933) when Ruth visited an orphanage to meet six boys who had helped stop a train from going into a washout. What was their wish? To meet Babe Ruth. He gave each of them an autographed baseball with an invitation to attend a Yankees game in New York.

'*THOUSANDS IN ALOHA TO BABE RUTH*' cries the top of page 1 in huge bold letters. That is from *The Honolulu Star-Bulletin* (October 19, 1933).

'*Babe Ruth Started on a Hunger Strike and The Umpire Called Him Out*' is the monster headline from *The New York Evening Journal* (January 13, 1926). Running across the page is a string of four photos depicting the alleged damage to his stomach after he had downed a dozen hot dogs which promptly put him in hospital. The second photo shows a shirtless Ruth and over his mid-section is a smaller shot of hot dogs — real hot dogs — and they are numbered 1 to 12. The caption for that one reads:

> '*Here are the twelve Hot Dogs that upset the stomach of the man who upset the batting records. Notice how snugly they nestle in the vast cavern of our Mr. Ruth's interior. Note how peaceful they look: how coy and shrinking. Surely, no trouble could follow in the wake of so comfy an array of edibles, it seems.*'

The photo right after that shows a glum Ruth sitting in his hospital bed.

One clipping even had the day-by-day/hour-by-hour schedule for his upcoming visit to the city, which in this case happened to be Providence, Rhode Island:

> *Monday, 1:18 P.M. — The World's Greatest Baseball Player arrives from Washington.*

> *Monday, 3:45 P.M. — The Idolized Bambino makes his first Providence appearance as a Keith Vaudeville headliner at the E.F. Albee Theatre.*

Monday: 4:45 P.M. — The Sultan of Swat receives delegation of newspaper men.

Monday, 6 P.M. — The Babe is the guest of honor at dinner at Crown Hotel given by prominent local business men and sportsmen.

Tuesday afternoon — The World-Famous Home Run Hero visits St. Aloysius Home to meet the youngsters of that institution, remembering his own youth in a Baltimore orphanage.

Tuesday evening — Brown Night. Baseball and Football Squads of Brown University, together with members of the student body and ladies, in theatre party.

Tuesday evening, 10 O'clock — Reception by Bishop Hickey and other prominent clergymen in honor of Babe Ruth at Cathedral Club.

And that was only for Monday and Tuesday. Ruth was clearly revered by one and all, and the clippings of the day really bring this home.

'*Why man he doth bestride the narrow world like a Colossus*' reads the caption from *The New York Evening Post* (October 12, 1928). The line is from Shakespeare's *Julius Caesar* (Act I, Scene II) where Cassius talks to Brutus, but this time it serves as the caption to a full-page drawing of Ruth standing astride the world — with a bat — and across the top he is dubbed '*The Modern Colossus.*' The artist was none other than cartoonist Robert LeRoy Ripley who would go on to fame as the creator of *Ripley's Believe It or Not!*

Another newspaper article in the collection, this from *The New York Times*, is about '*THE TWELVE GREATEST AMERICAN MEN — Selections Range from Leaders in Statecraft, Science, Industry, Literature and Art to Babe Ruth*' (July 23, 1922). Ruth is right up there with Thomas Edison, John D. Rockefeller, and Alexander Graham Bell. But what is notable even for this illustrious group is that his name is the only one that makes it into the headline.

If Ruth was celebrated by the masses, with kids it was on yet another level. An even higher level. The only word to describe it would be *Godly*.

'*Small Boys Mob Babe Ruth as he Hits Three Home Runs*' (*Trenton Evening Times*, October 12, 1927).

In one clipping there is a huge cartoon of Ruth doffing his cap while he is surrounded by a throng of admiring youngsters (*New Orleans Times-Picayune*, April 10, 1932). The caption reads: '*If kids could vote — a presidential possibility.*'

But the most telling thing from all these scrapbooks is not in the articles. It is in the photographs. There are countless photos — taken throughout his career — of Ruth visiting children in orphanages, hospitals, and other places where they aren't at home with family. And those kids come in all races, all ethnicities, all ages. It brings to mind a comment made by his widow Claire from her 1959 book *The Babe and I*:

> "He went to see more sick kids than any man who ever lived. And every visit tore him to pieces."[29]

Did Ruth have a soft spot in his heart for children? Indeed, the scrapbooks are more than telling. This is a letter he sent to a man named Henry Friedman in 1922:

> *Won't you help this youngster and hundreds of others like him who have no place to slam a ball except in the streets?*
>
> *The Playground Recreation and Association of America is constantly working to establish playgrounds where children need them most.*
>
> *Any contribution helps — $10 is a safe hit — $100 a home run. Let's keep the ball over the fence.*
>
> *Your check may be sent to me care of The Playground Recreation and Association of America, 1 Madison Avenue, New York City.*
>
> *Sincerely yours,*
> *"Babe" Ruth*

Another lesson from the scrapbooks is revealing about the endorsement power of Ruth's name. Says the headline above a shot of him standing in front of a car, along with two boys in overalls: *'Babe Ruth Uses Oldsmobile in Trek to Kids.'* There are full-page ads offering only Babe Ruth items for sale and Page 5 of *The Boston Post* from November 7, 1921 is a good example. Across the top of the page is his schedule for the next day in which he will visit eight business establishments in the city between 10 a.m. and 3:15 p.m. The headline says: *'CHAMPION HOME RUN HITTER AS SALESMAN.'* Below that are four ads. The first is for his appearance at a local hardware store. Then it is a clothing store where he will be in the flesh selling merchandise to customers. In another ad for yet another store he will be around to sell overcoats. The last ad is for a car — this time a Studebaker — and for thirty precious minutes he will be right in the showroom selling cars himself. Over the photo of Ruth and the car it says: *'Here's Babe Ruth and the Studebaker Car He Chose to Tour Boston in.'*

There is an ad for *'The BABE RUTH CAP for men and young men'* and another one for *'The BABE RUTH SWEATER for boys.'* And if you really like that sweater there is this: *'A baseball bat with Babe Ruth's personal signature will be given away with each order of TEN DOZEN or more of the Babe Ruth sweaters.'*

Along with all this is Babe Ruth the vaudeville star and Babe Ruth the movie star. One scrapbook includes a full-page promo from a magazine for a silent film he made in 1920. The film was called *'Headin' Home'* and the story line involves a small-town guy who becomes a baseball player. Babe, of course, plays himself. Across the top of the page it says *'Babe Ruth in "Headin' Home."'* The smaller print — which isn't really that small — cites *'That Record Breaking Feature Starring the Great Record Breaker'* and directly below is a photo of actor Ruth and his female lead, and the words *'A Romance of Youth and Happiness.'*

Make no mistake, this guy was the Big Deal. And he still is.

According to Jim Gates, Library Director at the National Baseball Hall of Fame and Museum, there are 590 biographies about Babe

Ruth that have been published in over 1,000 editions in multiple languages. And all of this is held in more than 58,000 libraries around the world.

Says Gates: "He was bigger than life and a legend was created around him, but he seems to be able to live up to the legend."

Jeff Idelson has been President of the Baseball Hall of Fame and Museum since 2008, but has been with the institution since 1994, initially as Director of Public Relations and Promotions, and later as Vice President of Communications and Education. Prior to joining the Hall he also had a four-year stint as Director of Media Relations and Publicity for The New York Yankees.

What does Ruth mean to Cooperstown? This is what Idelson says:

"When you talk about the history of baseball, you can't not include Babe Ruth. He's larger than life, and as we move further away from his playing days every year, his legacy doesn't shrink. It grows because of the lasting impact he had on the game. Ruth is one of just a handful of people whose name is synonymous with baseball. His legacy is profound. This is a guy that combined ability and stardom with a vast appreciation for the fans. They adored him and he allowed himself to adore them back."

Idelson went on.

"There is the old tongue-in-cheek joke that there are more balls signed by him in existence than *not* signed by him. That shows his appreciation for those who supported him and cared about him. He loved life and fans tend to gravitate to that endearing quality from superstars who embrace the public."

And that is just it. Babe Ruth embraced the fans as much as they embraced him. It's called love and in this case it was mutual.

"He was a cultural icon, not a sports icon."
— *Michael Gibbons, Director Emeritus and Historian,*
The Babe Ruth Birthplace Foundation

Chapter 5

THE BABE RUTH MUSEUM
AND JOURNEY OF MICHAEL GIBBONS

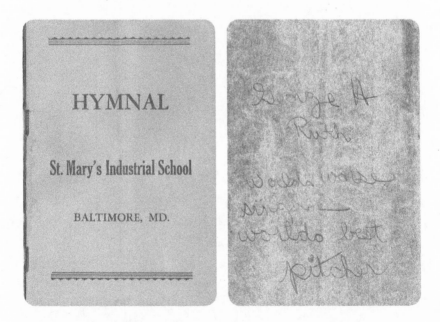

The first known Ruth autograph, believed to be signed when he was about twelve, was found in a book of hymns at St. Mary's Industrial School.

THE POPULAR 1960s TV show *Gilligan's Island* had a theme song that was widely recognized. As the song goes, seven people become castaways on an uncharted island after their boat is caught in a storm during what was supposed to have been 'a three-hour tour.' They wind up being stuck on the island for years. For Michael L. Gibbons, the journey into the life and legacy of Babe Ruth is something like that. What was supposed to have been a one-year contract turned out to last more than three decades.

It all started in 1981 when Baltimore native Gibbons was an independent documentary producer doing a feature on Babe Ruth. The production was funded by Mobil Oil and was to explore the early years of the young Ruth growing up in Baltimore with a focus on his burgeoning baseball prowess. In the process Gibbons interviewed a few old-timers who had actually played against Ruth in the sandlots of the city when the teenage Ruth was still a resident at St. Mary's Industrial School. This was before he became a professional baseball player.

"They told me that as a pitcher he was unhittable," says Gibbons, "and that as a hitter he could hit the ball farther than anyone and they really feared playing against him. This was when he was fourteen, fifteen, sixteen years old."

In the course of his research Gibbons visited the Babe Ruth Birthplace & Museum at 216 Emory Street. It had opened seven years earlier in 1974 and was ensconced in the very building where Ruth had been born on February 6, 1895. It was a small row house in a not-too-prosperous part of the city's downtown, not far from Oriole Park at Camden Yards where the major-league Baltimore Orioles play today. The home was leased by Ruth's grandfather on his mother's side. His name was Pius Schamberger.

Ruth's father George Sr. owned several saloons and one of them has a baseball connection. The place where it existed now sits in shallow center field at the aforementioned Oriole Park. Ruth's mother Kate had eight children, but only two of them — George Jr. and a girl, Mamie — would survive infancy. The children were all born in the same room — the grandparent's bedroom up on the second floor.

Gibbons has given the tour a thousand times.

When he was working on his documentary he got to know the caretaker of the museum and members of the board, and could see that the institution was struggling. According to Gibbons, it was "passively run" with only modest displays. He suggested they take a more aggressive approach to marketing.

A few years earlier, in the late 1960s, the building and three adjoining row houses had all been scheduled for demolition which prompted the office of the mayor to issue a press release. No way could the place where Babe Ruth was born be destroyed like this. The mayor was promptly flooded with mail, so he put together a committee and the city wound up purchasing the property. That led to a fundraising drive to restore the building and two key people became involved. One of them was Claire Ruth, the Babe's widow, and the other was Orioles' great Brooks Robinson, considered by many to be the best fielding third baseman ever.

In July, 1974 the Babe Ruth Birthplace and Shrine opened its doors. The Ruth family was involved through Claire — she would pass away two years later in 1976 — and the idea was to present the house as it was during the Babe's youth, along with a lot of artifacts. But in those early days the building was run by a person who worked only part-time. There was no executive director and no one running the show.

The documentary Gibbons made was never sold to a national outlet, but over the years it has been shown many times at the museum, and so have countless other productions Gibbons has done. He is, by trade, a producer of documentaries. It is no stretch to say that this

man may know more about Babe Ruth than anyone. Indeed, he is a walking encyclopedia of all things Ruthian, and as the person who led the museum for so many years, he is under no illusions about the mission of this institution.

"We are in the legacy business," he says.

Gibbons once interviewed a man who as a young boy had attended the very first induction ceremony in 1939 at the Baseball Hall of Fame and Museum in Cooperstown, New York. The man told Gibbons that Ruth was the only one of the inductees who got out and mixed with the crowd that day. And he also signed a lot of autographs.

When Gibbons was doing that documentary in 1981, he suggested the museum do a fundraiser and bring in some new exhibits. Inject a little blood into the place. He also had another idea. He said they should go beyond Ruth himself and expand the museum into a Baltimore baseball thing. And why not? Ruth had started his pro career with the minor-league Baltimore Orioles in 1914 and the major-league Orioles had no museum to recognize their past.

Nothing. Gibbons went to the front office of the Orioles with his plan and the team agreed to get involved.

A total of $265,000 was raised and the City of Baltimore put up funds, too. In November, 1982 the museum was closed for revamping and those new exhibits Gibbons wanted were brought in. The following May it opened again as the Babe Ruth Birthplace and Orioles Museum. That was when Gibbons was asked to take on the role of Executive Director, but he was still busy making documentary films. He decided he would do the job for one year and one year only. But, lo and behold, he would find that he enjoyed museum work. He enjoyed it a great deal.

Alas, that year turned out to be Gibbons 'three-hour tour.'

He personally handled all the films and audiovisuals for the museum, and still found time to do other documentaries on the side. But the museum would be his full-time job and it didn't take long for Gibbons to become a bone fide 'Babe Ruth nut.' He reasoned that the prime objective of a museum — any museum — is to tell stories and interpret those stories to the public. In this case, it just happened to be Babe Ruth's story.

Michael Gibbons

And what a story it was.

Gibbons has a B. A. from UMBC (University of Maryland, Baltimore County), and a master of Liberal Arts from Johns Hopkins University. He is a creative guy, and while he certainly knows much about baseball, there is a lot more to him than that. During all those years as Executive Director of the museum, Gibbons was also busy teaching a writing course in Baltimore.

"I taught this college writing course for twenty-seven years and every kid I ever taught knows who Babe Ruth is," he says, before stopping to correct himself. "Well the last year I taught it was in 2013 and there actually was one kid who didn't know who Babe Ruth was. He was from Nigeria."

Gibbons takes time out for a pause.

"That is the legacy. Today college kids don't know [world champion figure skater] Dorothy Hamill anymore. Two out of twenty know Dorothy. Only four out of twenty know Brooks Robinson which is just astonishing in this town."

Gibbons is shaking his head. A college student in Baltimore who has never heard of Brooks Robinson? Welcome to the 21st century.

"But everybody knows Babe Ruth," he says. "He did something through athletics which had never been seen before nor has it been seen since. He took the national pastime and turned it on its ear. He changed the way the game was played, the way the game was strategized. He was bigger than life playing on the world's biggest stage, New York City, and all the stars just lined up correctly, not to mention the fact that he understood the power of the media way back then. And he befriended the press which was a very smart thing to do. He had this endearing quality that the press loved which was that he was a twelve-year-old in an adult body. And he *loved* kids."

Gibbons waxes philosophic about Ruth and the state of the nation at that time. He says America grew up between the two world wars and that the country lived the rags-to-riches story just as Babe Ruth was living it in front of everyone's eyes.

"He just happened to be there. He just happened to be at the right place at the right time. All the time."

Gibbons mentions the 1918 World Series between the American League champion Boston Red Sox and National League champion Chicago Cubs. The Great War — World War I — was in its final days and U.S. President Woodrow Wilson thought it would be a good idea to honor wounded veterans at the first game. That game was played at Comiskey Park in Chicago and not Wrigley Field, home of the Cubs, because Comiskey had more seats. What's more, President Wilson suggested that *The Star Spangled Banner* be played when those veterans were being announced. The song was certainly well known, but it wasn't the official anthem just yet. It was played during the seventh-inning stretch.

"Who was warming up on the mound for the Red Sox when they played that song?" asks Gibbons. "Babe Ruth. That's who. He was there the very first time that song was played at a sporting event. They did it again for game two and when the series went back to Fenway Park in Boston they played the song before the first pitch and they've been doing it that way for sporting events ever since. And he was there the first time."

Gibbons takes out a newspaper — *The Baltimore Sun* from June 29, 2010. The lead story — 'A Ruthian Mystery' — was about Babe Ruth's minor-league rookie card from 1914. In 1914 he wasn't even known as the Babe. It was just George and he was a member of the minor-league Baltimore Orioles. The team's manager Jack Dunn had signed him as a 19-year-old pitcher right out of St. Mary's after seeing him pitch in a game the previous fall. The school was run by the Xaverian Brothers who had a policy of not releasing their 'inmates' until their 21st birthday. Dunn had to agree to sign legal guardian papers in order to get Ruth to spring training in Fayetteville, North Carolina. When he was there *The Baltimore Sun* began referring to him as "Jack Dunn's baby." In a few weeks that got shortened to 'Babe' and that is how the name began. And it stuck.

The museum had one of these old Ruth rookie cards on display, the property of an anonymous loaner, and the newspaper article concerned the identity of the person. The card, appraised to be in good condition, was estimated by *Forbes* to be worth $700,000. But Gibbons says the dollar value of the item is secondary to its worth as a *heritage* item, and as with everything Ruth touches, the value of that card has only gone up since then.

Babe Ruth rookie card

There are all kinds of artifacts on display at the museum, such as the scorebook from Ruth's first professional game with the Orioles, and the rosary he carried with him all his life. It also has the catcher's mitt and jersey which the young George had used when he was at St. Mary's Industrial School, and his very first known autograph, circa 1907. Ruth had signed his name in a book of hymns from the school, and one day it was discovered under the floorboards with an inscription, spelling mistake and all:

George H. Ruth, World's worse (sic) singer, world's best pitcher.

Ruth would have been about twelve at the time.

Then there are other things like the bat he once got from Shoeless 'Joe' Jackson when he was still with the Red Sox, along with countless other artifacts. The museum divides its exhibits, which are on display in 4,000 square feet of space, into six categories:

1. The Historic House, which is the actual building.

2. Babe Batted Here — artifacts from Ruth's early days at St. Mary's.

3. Babe: Husband, Father, Friend — family photos of Ruth and such items as the baseball from the legendary home run he hit for Johnny Sylvester, a little boy who was dying in hospital, and Ruth's radio from his New York apartment. He and Julia would listen to their favorite program — *The Lone Ranger* — every Sunday night.

4. The Ruthian Record — among other things a bat he had used from his 60-homer season in 1927, and the 'Player of the Century Award' bestowed by *Sports Illustrated*.

5. Ruth Starts 500 Home Run Club — a special display honoring all the members of this select group with Ruth as its 'founder.'

6. Playing the Babe — props and costumes from movies and TV programs about Ruth.

Over the years The Babe Ruth Birthplace & Museum has attracted well over one million visitors. For much of the time it was joined at the hip with the Sports Legends Museum, which celebrated local sports history including the old Baltimore Colts of the NFL, Baltimore's Orioles and Ravens, and other facets of Maryland's sports history. But Sports Legends Museum was forced to close its doors in 2015 after a new lease agreement could not be reached with the landlord, the Maryland Stadium Authority. As for the Babe Ruth side of things, the building underwent renovations from 2015 to 2017 and added such features as access for the disabled, including an elevator, not to mention new exhibits.

And so, the Babe Ruth Museum lives on. Just like Ruth.

In 2015 Major League Baseball produced a one-hour documentary called *American Hercules — Babe Ruth*. It was narrated by actor Martin Sheen. If you go to the www.imdb.com website this is what it says:

'The transformation of an incorrigible young boy into a global phenomenon named "The Babe." Babe Ruth's eternal stories and enduring star appeal remind us that truth is often greater than fiction.'

The documentary drew a parallel between the legendary Hercules and Ruth, and Gibbons was one of the people who was interviewed. What did Babe Ruth have in common with Hercules? Well, there were the twelve great labors performed by Hercules, one of which was slaying a lion. Ruth never slayed a lion, not literally, but finding a dozen myth-like things about him isn't hard to do. Especially for a man like Gibbons.

He launches into the exercise and speaks very quickly. He starts with the Called Shot Home Run from the 1932 World Series, and then the 'Hell with Babe Ruth' cry from Japanese troops in World War II, the home run hit for little Johnny Sylvester when he was dying in hospital, and a long list of other things from the life and times of the great Bambino.

It is easy and natural for Gibbons to wade into a discussion about Ruth the icon and how the phenomenon goes well beyond baseball.

"Babe Ruth has crossed over ... transcended sport... moved from the world of baseball to become an American cultural icon along with Marilyn Monroe and JFK and Martin Luther King and Elvis Presley and Abraham Lincoln," he says. "There are just a few names from our whole history where people have transcended out of wherever they made their celebrity and plopped into this iconic state that Babe enjoys. He is a cultural icon, not a sports icon. The legacy of Babe Ruth continues which is astonishing because that doesn't happen often. He instigated the legacy and it has been perpetuated."

Gibbons goes as far as calling Ruth "the Mount Rushmore of cultural icons." He says he probably signed more autographs than anybody and that to this day he has the most recognizable and valued autograph *in the world*.

"You tell me a more recognizable autograph," says Gibbons. "I mean is Abe Lincoln as well known as Ruth in Japan? I don't think so."

Gibbons tells a story about Mel Allen, whom he actually knew. Allen got involved with the Yankees in the 1940s when Ruth was ill and would drive him around the city as his personal chauffeur. Gibbons said Allen told him how Ruth always mixed with the crowd and always had time for everyone, no matter who they were.

He says Ruth remains the most famous sports icon ever and maybe, just maybe, the most famous American. He talks about his legacy not only in the United States and Canada, but throughout the Caribbean, Asia, the Far East. Anywhere baseball is played. And even places where it isn't.

Gibbons' 'three-hour tour' would run over thirty-five years and conclude — sort of — in February, 2017 when he formally retired as Executive Director of the Babe Ruth Birthplace & Museum. But he remained as Director Emeritus and Historian for The Babe Ruth Birthplace Foundation. The foundation is an independent, not-for-profit educational institution that perpetuates the sports heritage of

Maryland. In this capacity Gibbons still oversees all curatorial, archival and exhibits. It is a job that keeps him busy three days a week and then some.

The museum has been left in good hands with Shawn M. Herne who now serves as its second ever Executive Director. But Herne is anything but a newcomer to the place. He spent twelve years working with Gibbons as Chief Curator and is an integral part of the cultural heritage of both the city of Baltimore and the state of Maryland. Herne is a member of the Board of Directors of the Maryland Museum Association and of the Mid-Atlantic Association of Museums. For eight years he served on the board of the International Sports Heritage Association, a non-profit organization that assists and promotes sport museums and halls of fame. More than 130 institutions from North America, South America, Europe and Asia are members.

In addition to its full-time staff, the Babe Ruth Birthplace & Museum has its own Board of Directors and an Advisory Council. The Advisory Council includes such people as Ruth's grandson Tom Stevens.

And what about St. Mary's Industrial School for Boys, where Ruth first learned to play baseball? St. Mary's closed in 1950 and became the site of the all-boys Cardinal Gibbons School (no relation to Michael Gibbons), but that institution would close its doors in 2010. However, the original building and baseball field have been preserved. In 2012 the property was purchased and redeveloped into affordable housing for low-income residents. And that sits pretty well with Michael Gibbons who reasons that the baseball field had to be saved. There was no way around it.

"This is hallowed ground," he says. "Like Gettysburg."

"Babe Ruth was so big in his day and it's just carried over from generation to generation. He's still out there."

— Steve Tellefsen, President & CEO, Babe Ruth League Inc.

Chapter 6

MORE THAN A MILLION STRONG

THE YARDVILLE HOTEL in Hamilton, New Jersey has been around a long time. It was once known as the Yardville Inn and there are records about a building dating as far back as 1799. That was the year when George Washington died and his successor John Adams was serving as the second president of the young republic. The vice president was a man named Thomas Jefferson.

Over the years the name of the hotel has changed — from The Inn at Sand Hills to the Yardville Roadhouse and then to the Old Yardville Inn. Of course, this was all during the days of the horse and buggy. The stage coach used to stop right at the front door to unload passengers and those passengers included such people as theater actress May Yohé whose biggest claim to fame was coming into possession of an item of notable jewellery after she had married Lord Francis Hope in 1894. The jewellery was none other than the world-famous Hope Diamond which is now on display at the Smithsonian Museum of Natural History in Washington, D.C. Its value is estimated at $350 million.

In the early 1900s the Old Yardville Inn became known as the Yardville Hotel and the name hung on. And the famous people kept coming. It is said that sharpshooter Annie Oakley and William Frederic Cody, who was better known as Buffalo Bill, visited on at least one occasion when they were busy touring the country as headliners of the fabled Buffalo Bill's Wild West show.

Today the establishment is no longer a hotel, but remains as the Yardville Inn Wine, Spirits, Restaurant & Tavern, and it is still a popular place for people to get together for dinner and drinks. Perhaps the most auspicious meeting that ever occurred at the Yardville Hotel happened on February 9, 1951. It was a time when a postage stamp cost three cents and a gallon of gas nineteen cents, and coast-to-coast telephone service by direct-dial was just beginning. What happened that day was that ten local men from the community gathered to talk baseball, but not professional baseball. It was about a problem that existed at the time for boys aged thirteen to fifteen.

While there was Little League ball for boys who were younger than thirteen and organized ball under the umbrella of the American Legion Junior Baseball Program for those over fifteen, boys in the 13-to-15 age group were left out in the cold and caught in a gap. A void. They had nowhere to play. And so, these ten men decided to do something about it. They formed the Little Bigger League.

The man recognized as the founding father of the program was Marius D. Bonacci, and the other nine were: Samuel M. Welch, Ferdinand J. Wagner, Ed Jones, Ted Jaskek, Cliff Fovour, Boots Snyder, William Dombrowski, Maskill Paxson, and Willard Carson, Jr. Carson would serve as president of the first Little Bigger League.

Carson was a locomotive engineman on Conroil — it was called the Pennsylvania Railroad and Penn Central in those days — and was so inspired by the boys playing baseball and the crowds showing up to watch them that he decided to write about it for the *Sporting News*. In his article Carson said he was looking for interested parties who wanted to organize baseball leagues and join this new organization that he was leading. Within a year some ninety-eight municipalities across the United States had responded to his offer.

Carson would retire from his railway job in 1978 after thirty-seven years of service and he died in 2008 as the last living founder of that baseball organization. But his hard work and inspiration continue to live on.

In that first summer the Little Bigger League operated in two divisions, aptly named the American Division and National Division. Before long word got out and pretty soon more towns wanted to get involved. Sponsors joined in, most notably Coca-Cola and Bottlers of Coco-Cola, and both of them agreed to help make this a true national movement. The Little Bigger League incorporated and registered as a

Former Babe Ruth League President Cliff Conner,
center, with members of the Executive Staff outside the first
Babe Ruth League Headquarters in Trenton, New Jersey.

non-profit organization that was determined to further the development of American youth through baseball.

And it did.

The first World Series championship was held in Stamford, Connecticut with teams coming from all over the country and beyond. There were applications from Puerto Rico, Canada, Cuba, Alaska — it wasn't a state yet — and from as far away as London and Paris. With Coca-Cola still on as chief sponsor, the league advertised in *Sporting News Magazine*, which was the bible of baseball in America. It wasn't long before one hundred baseball *leagues* were involved.

Then, in 1954, the Little Bigger League approached Babe Ruth's widow Claire with an idea. The league wanted to change the name of this growing, but still fledgling organization, to Babe Ruth League and asked for her permission. She said yes and thought the Babe would have liked that sort of thing. To this day the official program still retains a quote from Claire:

> "Babe was a man who loved children and baseball. He could receive no greater tribute than to have a youth baseball program named after him."

But why Babe Ruth League?

Robert P. Flaherty, Jr., who is the long-time Vice President and Commissioner, Babe Ruth League, replies: "What name would you pick that was more iconic? This is the guy who saved the game of baseball."

Claire Ruth's generous gift lit the fuse that would ignite the growth and development of Babe Ruth League, Inc. After the name change, growth of the organization went into high gear. This was only a few short years after Ruth's death — he had died in 1948 — and the fathers and grandfathers of all those boys aged thirteen to fifteen were still fresh with memories of the great Bambino. And some of them had even seen him play.

In 1966, Babe Ruth League took the next step up the baseball ladder for young athletes. This was the Babe Ruth 16-18 Division. So now boys up to the age of eighteen could play under the Babe Ruth banner. Eight years after that, in 1974, the 13-Year-Old Prep League was added which allowed 13-year-old players to make the transition to a regulation-size diamond and compete with peers their own age. In 1982, Babe Ruth League added yet another division to its program, the Bambino Division for players aged four to twelve.

But what about girls? They wanted to play baseball, too. Babe Ruth League saw an obvious need for a quality national softball program for young female athletes, and in 1984 Babe Ruth Softball got off the ground with divisions for girls aged four to eighteen.

In 1999 a new era was launched for Babe Ruth League as the Bambino division was renamed Cal Ripken Baseball. Cal Ripken, Jr. — baseball's iron man who broke the consecutive-games record of

Left to right: Robert Flaherty, Vice President and Commissioner, Babe Ruth League; Steve Tellefsen, President & CEO, Babe Ruth League; Hall of Famer Cal Ripken, Jr.; Rob Manfred, Commissioner, Major League Baseball; and James Wagoner, Chairman, Babe Ruth League Board of Directors. Photo was taken in 2016 at the Cal Ripken World Series which is a division of Babe Ruth League.

Lou Gehrig —was himself a player in the Babe Ruth League program when he was a boy. The idea was that the visions and philosophies of Cal Ripken, Sr., both as a player and coach, and those of his sons Cal, Jr., and Billy, parallel those of Babe Ruth League. And what were those visions and philosophies? To provide every youngster with the opportunity to play baseball and have fun doing it.

In 1999 Cal Ripken, Jr. was still one of the biggest stars in Major League Baseball. That season he hit .340 for the Baltimore Orioles. He retired two years later, having been an All-Star for twenty consecutive seasons.

Cal Ripken Baseball consists of a major division for players aged ten to twelve and a minor division for those who are nine and ten. Then there is the Rookie group for seven- and eight-year-olds. This division uses a pitching machine to lob balls at the batter. Finally, the T-Ball division is for the youngest group of all — four- to six-year-olds — and for them the batter hits the ball from a batting tee adjusted to the player's height.

In 2007 Babe Ruth League introduced something new — the Cal Ripken Major/70 Division. Cal Ripken Baseball leagues would now have the option of offering a Cal Ripken Major/60 program or a Cal Ripken Major/70 program, or both, to their young athletes. In the Cal Ripken Major/70 Division the pitcher's mound was fifty feet from home plate and the base paths were seventy feet long which are less than the dimensions for a regular baseball diamond. The Cal Ripken Major/60 Division had smaller dimensions still in order to accommodate those who were just learning the game. The pitcher's mound was forty-six feet from home plate and the base paths sixty feet long.

Players were introduced to a regulation-size diamond — pitcher's mound is sixty feet and six inches from home plate, and base paths ninety feet between bases — at the age of thirteen. The idea behind all this was that kids would grow with the game.

It was none other than Babe Ruth himself who said as much in that famous speech he delivered when he was in failing health at Yankee Stadium on April 27, 1947. It was Babe Ruth Day. Ironically, he was introduced that day by a 13-year-old boy and this is what he said:

"Thank you very much, ladies and gentlemen. You know how bad my voice sounds, well it feels just as bad. You know this baseball game of ours comes up from the youth. That means the boys. And after you're a boy and grow up to know how to play ball, then you come to the boys you see representing themselves today in your national pastime. The only real game, I think, in the world is baseball.

As a rule some people think if you give them a football or a baseball or something like that, naturally they're athletes right away. But you can't do that in baseball. You've got to start from way down at the bottom when you're six or seven years of age. You can't wait until you're fifteen or sixteen. You've got to let it grow up with you. And if you're successful and you try hard enough you're bound to come out on top. Just like these boys have come to the top now."

Ruth, who would die the following year, could have been writing the mission statement for the organization that would one day bear his name. He was known as an all-inclusive guy, a man who crossed the color line at a time when it wasn't done, and who was open to all kinds of people, no matter their background or situation in life.

In the year 2000 Babe Ruth League took this notion to heart with the formation of the Buddy-Ball Division for players aged five to twenty who were physically or mentally challenged. Why buddy? A 'buddy' helps the player swing a bat, round the bases, or catch a ball.

The point was that baseball is for everyone.

And for those girls who were more bent on the competitive edge, in 2013 the league started Xtreme Fastpitch. This division would be for softball players who want to play at a recreational level or a higher level of competition, and then go on to play in high school and beyond.

Babe Ruth League is built on the concept of inclusiveness and providing all its players with life lessons that extend beyond the baseball field. It prides itself on being a youth leadership organization, as well as a competitive baseball and softball program.

Today Babe Ruth League, Inc., a non-profit educational organization, ranks as one of the premier youth baseball and softball organizations in the world. In 2005 the number of total participants went over the one-million mark. In addition to that, there is a dedicated volunteer network of close to two million people. These are people with jobs, families, and many other commitments, but they freely give their time and resources. Add it all up and you have *three million people* involved in Babe Ruth League.

According to official population stats, only a few cities in the United States have more than three million people living in the core — starting with New York City and Los Angeles. Take all the people involved in Babe Ruth League and you would have one of America's largest cities!

Babe Ruth League has grown — mushroomed — to an entity with over one million players who play on more than 56,000 teams in almost 10,000 leagues.

The Babe Ruth International Board is the organization's governing body while Babe Ruth League International Headquarters at 1670 Whitehorse-Mercerville Road in Hamilton Township, New Jersey, serves as the administrative and promotional center. There is a full-time staff of fifteen employees, as well as interns who assist during different times of the year.

Then there is the Babe Ruth League Alumni Association, a separate entity from Babe Ruth League, which advances the general welfare of Babe Ruth League, Inc. and helps the organization prepare its players to meet the challenges of adolescence and adulthood, not to mention encourage their drive for excellence and achievement.

The Babe Ruth League Alumni Association provides two scholar-ships that offer financial assistance to former players from Cal Ripken Baseball, Babe Ruth Baseball, and Babe Ruth Softball who are look-ing to further their education beyond high school. These scholarships are the Babe Ruth League Alumni College Scholarship and the Irby Luquette Endowed College Scholarship. The late Irby Luquette of Abbeville, Louisiana gave almost sixty years of service to Babe Ruth League in a variety of positions. Another scholarship for former soft-ball players is named after the late Jaime Lynn Horn, a woman who served as Babe Ruth Softball National Commissioner.

Baseball's World Series is a competition between the champions of the American League and National League, and aside from the one Canadian team in Major League Baseball, there is nothing interna-tional about it at all. Not so with the Babe Ruth League World Series. In fact, this is very much an international thing.

The way things are set up is that a tournament team from each chartered local league enters its district tournament. District win-ners then advance to state-wide competition, with the winning team qualifying for one of eight regional tournaments. The eight regions are: New England, Middle Atlantic, Ohio Valley, Southeast, Midwest Plains, Southwest, Pacific Northwest and Pacific Southwest. The eight regional champions compete in each World Series.

Babe Ruth League, Inc. has grown from its inaugural 13-15 World Series in 1952 to seven baseball and six softball World Series. The full list includes: Cal Ripken 10-Year-Old, Cal Ripken Major/60, Cal Ripken Major/70, 13-Year-Old, 14-Year-Old, 13-15, 16-18, Softball 8U, Softball 10U, Softball 12U, Softball 14U, Softball 16U and Softball 18U World Series.

The Cal Ripken Major/70 World Series features eight to sixteen teams from the U.S. and also eight international teams (outside the U.S.) to determine a true World Champion.

No matter how one cuts it, millions of kids have benefited from their involvement in Babe Ruth League, and the alumni include some recognizable names starting with none other than Michael Jordan, who is widely considered the greatest basketball player in history. Growing up in Wilmington, North Carolina, Jordan played Babe Ruth League baseball. (He also interrupted his storied NBA career to play minor-league baseball for a few seasons). In the book The Jordan Rules by Sam Smith (Pocket Books, a division of Simon Schuster, New York 1993), Jordan said: "Even now, when people talk about my greatest thrill being the shot against Georgetown to win the NCAA title, I still think to myself that my greatest accomplishment really is the Most Valuable Player Award I got when my Babe Ruth League team won the state baseball championship."[30]

Another famous alumnus is Peyton Manning, one of the greatest NFL quarterbacks ever, who played in the program in his native New Orleans, Louisiana.

As for baseball Hall of Famers, the list of alumni is a long one. It includes Carl Yastrzemski, Joe Morgan, Jim Palmer, Rod Carew, Steve Carlton, George Brett, Nolan Ryan, Carlton Fisk, Eddie Murray, Paul Molitor, Ryne Sandberg, Rickey Henderson, Jim Rice, Frank Thomas, John Smoltz, Randy Johnson, Mike Piazza and, of course,

Cal Ripken, Jr. Yastrzemski, who was voted to the Hall of Fame at Cooperstown in 1989, has the honor of being the very first Babe Ruth League graduate to achieve that distinction.

In addition to that are current major-league players who will likely have a place in Cooperstown. This group includes such players as Dustin Pedroia, Mookie Betts, and Mike Trout. Trout, who in his younger days played in Babe Ruth League in Millville, New Jersey, was a pitcher of all things and became known as the *Millville Meteor*.

A pitcher who became a slugger? Shades of Babe Ruth!

Babe Ruth League has also involved famous personalities from beyond the world of sport. Film and TV actress Rhonda Fleming, who made more than forty films and was a big star in the 1940s and 1950s, was once Treasurer of the Beverly Hills, California league. Legendary entertainer Bob Hope was President of the Toluca, California league for three years in the late '50s and his wife Dolores was Secretary. Actor Tom Selleck excelled as a pitcher in Sherman Oaks, California when he was a boy. When singer Bruce Springsteen — *the Boss* — was growing up in Freehold Borough, New Jersey, he too played in the local Babe Ruth league; his song *Blinded by the Light* with its reference to 'Indians in the summer' actually refers to the name of his youth baseball team. Of more recent vintage there is TV host Jimmy Fallon who played Babe Ruth League baseball in Saugerties, New York.

All of them are Babe Ruth League alumni.

Steve Tellefsen has been President and CEO of the Babe Ruth League since April, 2005. That was when he took over from his father Ron. Ron died in March of that year and had led the organization since 1980. A quarter of a century. During those twenty-five years under Ron, the number of players in the program went from 350,000 to over one million. Ron, who worked for the United States Post Office in his day job, got started as an umpire for the league's World Series in the early 1960s before becoming a National Commissioner and then President which, of course, was a full-time job.

Ron was a man who, just like the Babe himself, loved kids. He believed that youth baseball and softball were the perfect venues for teaching the game of life.

With his expertise in umpiring, Ron founded the Babe Ruth League National Umpires Association to improve the quality of umpiring at the local league level by educating men and women in the rules and mechanics of the game. Ron was also credited with the permanent inclusion of Babe Ruth League, Inc. as part of the estate of Babe Ruth. In addition, he was one of two representatives from amateur baseball who served on the Advisory Board of the Major League Baseball Rules Committee.

Steve Tellefsen is no stranger to youth sports. The game of baseball has been part of his entire life — from playing Babe Ruth Baseball in his youth, to traveling to Babe Ruth events with his father, to umpiring as an adult. Once he even met Claire Ruth at a state fair. She presented him with a signed baseball — *Mrs. Babe Ruth* — and he still has it.

"My Dad was a hard-working man who traveled extensively but he always made time for his family," says Steve. "There were so many activities we did together and one of my favorite was playing golf with him. He was such a competitor on the golf course. I also enjoyed accompanying him to New York to play in card games with his old buddies. All of them were dedicated to the game of baseball."

Steve says his father was always involved in baseball — first as a young bat boy, then as a player and later as a manager. But he says Ron's first love was really umpiring.

"It wasn't the money that attracted him to umpiring. It was his love for the game and respect for the rules."

While it was his father's wish that he join the Babe Ruth organization after completing high school, Steve decided instead to attend college and explore other things. He joined the United States Marine Corps where he spent four years. Steve says the marines instilled in him the qualities of "inner and outer strength," as well as a foundation that would serve him well in life.

When he returned from military duty, he joined the United Parcel Service where he worked for thirteen years before taking time off for a medical issue. During this time an opening developed in the mailroom at Babe Ruth League Headquarters and he decided to take the position.

Then, when a National Commissioner position opened, Steve was advanced to the job and ran four regions — New England, Southeast, Southwest, and Midwest Plains. After his father passed away, the Board of Directors elected Steve to lead the organization. Since then many technological advancements have come under him, along with the launch of the Cal Ripken Major/70 and Xtreme Fastpitch Divisions. This required education and certification of coaches, and nationwide background checks. Also under Steve came the addition of three Softball World Series and more international World Series activity.

Babe Ruth League operates with an annual budget of about $4 million and assists with the administration of some seventy-two state organizations and almost 10,000 leagues. One of the main priorities is to keep the costs for joining as low as possible. How low?

The cost for registering *an entire team* ranges from $15 to $30, depending on the age group. How do they do that?

"We identify and implement all possible cost-reduction measures," Steve says. "Our volunteers rely heavily on the services and products offered by Babe Ruth League, so we work hard to present them with a wide array of sponsors. These sponsors are prominent names in the youth sports industry. This assists with raising funds and saving money on uniforms, equipment and other necessary essentials."

That means such companies as Rawlings, BSN Sports, Louisville Slugger, Under Armour, Franklin Sports, and Majestic Athletic are involved, as are many others. Babe Ruth League also partners with Human Kinetics which is the leading provider of youth, high school and elite-level sport education programs in the country. The idea is to develop good coaches and managers in order to keep the experience for all participants in Babe Ruth League fun and educational.

And it all comes back to Babe Ruth himself.

Left to right: Rick Dell, Director of Major League Baseball Development, Asia; Weiwei Gao, General Manager, Le Sports China; and Steve Tellefsen, President & CEO, Babe Ruth League. They are shown with the statue of Babe Ruth at Babe Ruth International Headquarters in Hamilton, New Jersey.

Says Steve: "Babe Ruth was larger than life. He embodied all the qualities that a sport-loving nation demanded of an outstanding hero. Stories and some myths about the Babe have been shared from generation to generation. And his legend lives on. The Babe is still around us in literature, art, movies and music. It's as if he retired only yesterday.

"In our organization we are proud to perpetuate that name. Babe Ruth loved and cared about the well-being of kids and that's what we're about. We are a place to play baseball and softball, but we're also a place where kids learn life's lessons — teamwork, respect for people from all walks of life, a sense of family and community, learning from mistakes, dealing gracefully with losing and winning, just to name a few. I think if Babe Ruth was live today he would be ecstatic and very proud of the traditions, morals and ethics endorsed by the organization that bears his name."

But it hasn't always been easy. Steve Tellefsen is the first to admit that young boys and girls don't automatically gravitate to baseball the way they once did, not with so many other sports and so many options available to them nowadays. There is competition. A lot of competition. But still, thousands of children and youths flock to Babe Ruth League fields each year, eager to play. And the Ruth family stays involved.

For example, both Julia Ruth Stevens and her son Tom Stevens attend Babe Ruth League events. In fact, Steve says Julia used to be a "regular on the tour," and as recently as 2016 she attended a Babe Ruth World Series. She was 100 years old at the time. But it was Claire, Julia's mother, who first got the thing going.

On August 16, 1961 — the thirteenth anniversary of Ruth's death — it was Babe Ruth League Day at Yankee Stadium and Claire was the special guest. She picked a good day to appear. That day Roger Maris went 3 for 4 at the plate with two home runs — nos. 47 and 48 — on his way to hitting sixty-one and breaking Ruth's single-season record of sixty which had stood since 1927. Thirty-four years. Of course, as most everyone knows, Maris did his thing in a 162-game season while Ruth's feat had been accomplished in a shorter 154-game season. And so, Maris was destined to live the rest of his life with that famous asterisk beside his great achievement.

What does the future hold for Babe Ruth League?

In 2015 the organization moved into spanking new headquarters in Hamilton, New Jersey after outgrowing its long-time facility in Trenton, New Jersey. Steve Tellefsen says there were three storage facilities full of historical documents, player rosters and memorabilia involved in that move. The new headquarters plays host to a state-of-the-art Hall of Fame and Museum Room that greets visitors as they enter through the main door. This room, which features a life-size statue of the Babe, also contains many pieces of memorabilia involving Babe Ruth and famous alumni.

Two relatively recent developments — the Babe Ruth League digital data center and Babe Ruth Online — have been a big success for Babe Ruth League, Inc., and its member leagues and commissioners. The Data Center makes it easy for leagues to register and insure their programs online in a matter of minutes, while the full-service technology of Babe Ruth Online allows volunteers to manage a wide range of activities with the click of a button.

The League also has its own online store where one can purchase team accessories and umpire supplies — everything from bats and balls and caps to hoodies and short-sleeve jerseys — with the organization's logo front and center. What's more, everything can be bought online at any time night or day by visiting www.baberuthleague.org. The website also provides visitors access to such resources as the President's Handbook with everything there is to know about Babe Ruth League, as well as information about chartering and insurance, how to run your own program, and access to the League's informative e-newsletters which are called *Batter Up, Commissioners Corner* and *UmpireGram.*

Steve, who logs a great many miles for Babe Ruth League in his job as President & CEO, says 'travel baseball' is becoming very popular and the League is researching new ways to accommodate all baseball players — from those who want to play on a recreational level to those who seek a higher degree of competition.

He says he looks forward to expanding Babe Ruth League's international presence and points out that teams from Australia, Canada, the Dominican Republic, Japan, Korea, Mexico, New Zealand, and Puerto Rico regularly take part in the Cal Ripken Major/70 World Series for 12-year-olds. In 2017, a girls' softball team from Beijing, China competed in the Babe Ruth Softball 12U World Series in Jensen Beach, Florida.

In the fall of 1934 Babe Ruth visited Japan with a team of American League All-Stars to play a series of exhibition games, and to say he was a big hit is putting it mildly. On that trip he also took part in a game that was played in Shanghai, China, so what goes around comes around.

Says Steve Tellefsen: "We keep the Babe Ruth name out there more than anybody and we're going to keep on doing it."

*"He was an overwhelmingly positive figure, and from
a licensing perspective for a sports legend, he is at the very top.
He has not only survived, but he has thrived."*
— Pete Enfield, Partner and President, Luminary Group LLC

Chapter 7

WHAT'S IN A NAME

Babe Ruth was the first American to be featured on
the Boeing 787 Dreamliner aircraft for Norwegian.

"**B**ABE RUTH is our biggest client," says Pete Enfield, and he's a man who knows a thing or two about the merchandising power of deceased celebrities.

Enfield is a Partner and President of Luminary Group LLC, which is a leading intellectual management company. Based in Indiana, it represents big names from the worlds of sports, music and entertainment. While Ruth is the company's no. 1 account in sports licensing, he is, as Enfield says, also the company's biggest account.

In addition to Ruth, Luminary represents the likes of such baseball greats as Satchel Paige, Walter Johnson, Honus Wagner, and Cy Young. Other noted clients are football star Johnny Unitas, golf's Sam Snead, Olympic star Jesse Owens, college football coach Knute Rockne, and pro football coach Vince Lombardi. Lombardi is Luminary's second biggest client after Ruth. The firm also has clients from other fields such as actor Bob Denver and famed cyclist Marshall 'Major' Taylor. There is good reason why all these deceased celebrities are represented. They are in demand, some more than others.

Enfield is a lawyer who grew up a sports junkie. He was born in California and then the family moved to New Orleans where his father worked in the athletics department at Tulane University. Basketball and football were the big sports around there, and Enfield spent many an evening taking in basketball games on campus or going to the Superdome with his family to watch sporting events. Growing up, he shadowed his three older brothers everywhere they went, begging to participate in their games and activities. When he was eleven, the family moved again, this time to northern Indiana which was a stark contrast to the warmth and humidity of Louisiana, but Enfield's love of sports did not wane. He graduated with a degree in Sports

Marketing from Indiana University-Bloomington, and later received his Juris Doctor from the University of Dayton School of Law.

In the early 1990s Enfield got involved with Babe Ruth, or to be more accurate, the family of Babe Ruth. It was 1994 when he embarked on a career in the entertainment business, first as a law clerk and then as Senior Vice President with CMG Worldwide, the company representing Ruth and other deceased celebrities at the time. CMG was one of the leading companies in establishing licensing opportunities for iconic personalities.

The year 1995 was the 100th anniversary of the birth of Babe Ruth which created a unique marketing opportunity. Back then the business of licensing famous people after their deaths was still in its infancy, but the centennial of Ruth was something special. Here was a long-dead, but still widely celebrated figure who was charismatic, outgoing, charitable — and most important of all — universally loved and admired. Of course, he was best known for hitting home runs and that meant strength and power, not to mention the fact that he did this for a long time, so sustainability also comes into play. These were all key ingredients that could be attached to a whole slew of things in the world of marketing. But 1995 was a whole century after the man's arrival and almost a half-century after his death. Yet, he was still very much out there.

In short, Ruth was lasting. He had a *brand*.

He had already been associated with such companies as IBM. As early as 1989, IBM had been using a shot of Ruth with a computer on his lap in an ad that said '*All our heavy hitters are on sale.*' But there was also a Ruth connection to IBM from much earlier than that, albeit a tenuous one, and it does demonstrate the long-term durability and marketability of the Bambino.

The 1939 World's Fair was held in New York City and one of the days — May 4 — was designated as International Business Machines Day. This was four years after Ruth had retired as a player. That day — May 4, 1939 — he had signed his name to a ticket cover for a booklet containing passes and coupons for the World's Fair. All he did was scribble his name on it. But in 2017, some seventy-eight years later, that signed ticket cover sold in an online auction for $2,151. Such is the power of a celebrity and personality like Babe Ruth.

Over the years many companies have chosen to become involved with Ruth. Sears was one. Another was Coca-Cola which had been associated with him back in his playing days. But 1995 — the centennial of his birth — would be a big year for corporate America to get on board and a lot of companies did just that.

That year a bank in Pennsylvania used Ruth to link an older generation to its special checking options for people who were over the age of fifty-five. A company involved in power supplies used his likeness because, according to one executive, he conveyed a unique brand of nostalgic power. A line of children's apparel used him for a licensing program to bring the legends of yesterday to young people of the present day.

Then there was The Bradford Exchange. The company had been founded in 1973 as a trading center for collector's plates. Make that limited-edition, collector's plates. The key words behind these items are right up there on the company's website — *artistry, innovation and enduring value.* In 1995 The Bradford Exchange had a commemorative porcelain plate of Babe Ruth's Called Shot Home Run from the 1932 World Series. At the time The Bradford Exchange had sixteen Hall of Fame commemorative baseball plates on the market, involving such greats as Ty Cobb, Lou Gehrig, and of more recent vintage, Harmon Killebrew. But in 1995 sales of the Babe Ruth commemorative plate accounted for almost half of the company's sales of its entire line of commemorative plates.

All in all, retail sales of Babe Ruth items in that centennial year amounted to a cool $25 million.

Over the years, both before 1995 and since, a great many companies have attached themselves to Ruth and his *brand.* The list includes Pepsi which did a popular animation ad for TV for its Lipton Iced

Tea drink. The ad featured Ruth along with Reggie Jackson, George Steinbrenner, Billy Martin, and Mickey Mantle. The story line of the ad has Ruth sweating and sluggish at the plate until Jackson gives him the iced tea. Then the Bambino goes on to smash a home run, so this one is all about *power*.

Another company with a TV ad was Mercedes Benz. In this case it was a thirty-second spot that began with Babe Ruth and said how he had been acquired for $125,000. Then the spot moved on to how Alaska had been purchased for two cents an acre, and then how the world's first computer had cost $486,804.22.

"It isn't always what you pay," say the words as shots of the Mercedes come across the screen. "It's what you get in return." Then comes the big word and that's what this ad is all about.

VALUE.

So Babe Ruth represents something more than a baseball player who hit lots of home runs. Much more. He also represents power, value, and artistry, and if you want to crank down to an even deeper level we can add to the mix such qualities as humanity, decency and this almost God-like aura about him.

Enfield rhymes off the names of organizations — and these are only a small representation of the total — that have been attached to the Ruth juggernaut over the years and it seems never-ending.

Sony. Video games.

Chevrolet. The Called Shot Home Run from the 1932 World Series recreated by Little Leaguers.

Bud Light. The Called Shot Home Run is recreated yet again, but this time with actual footage of Ruth pointing to the outfield.

Boeing. A campaign to celebrate the company's 100th anniversary that uses three celebrities — Elvis Presley, Martin Luther King and Babe Ruth.

Jockey International. Multiple creative concepts for the company's 'Supporting Greatness' and 'Real Every Day' campaigns.

American Mint. Sculpted coins and baseballs.

The Bradford Exchange. Clocks, figurines, plates, trains, ornaments, and glove figurines.

Hanover Insurance. Print ads in *The Wall Street Journal*, in trade publications, in a brochure, and on the Web.

Kia Motors. Use of Babe's signature in a TV campaign.

Knights of Columbus. A five-year, TV campaign highlighting Babe's own membership in the KofC.

Anheuser Busch. The 'Always There' ad campaign.

Nestlé. The licensed use of Babe in a campaign for Baby Ruth.

And Coors Light, Absolut Vodka, Visa, Citibank, Nike, Adidas, what have you.

Then there are other companies, many of them leaders in their industries. A good example is Majestic Athletic which is the official on-field uniform of Major League Baseball. The company designs, markets and manufactures athletic apparel, team uniforms, outerwear and licensed athletic wear. One of the things it sells is a vintage 1927 New York Yankees jersey with RUTH and a big number '3' on the back.

As for others, here is a partial list:

Artissimo Designs. Canvas wall art and plaques.

Vilmain. Paperweights.

Pro Merch. Apparel.

Elemetal Minting. Copper round coins.

Copasetic Clothing and Roots of Fight. T-shirts, sweatshirts, sweatpants, tank tops, sweaters and hats.

Mitchell & Ness. Authentic replica jerseys.

Ripple Junction. T-shirts sold in Old Navy stores.

Open Road Brands. Wall art, metal signs and magnets.

Long Ball Licorice. Packaging for licorice products.

BR3 Enterprises. Babe-inspired condiments for the likes of barbecue sauce and relish.

CyberX. Mobile video game.

Mounted Memories. Framed and unframed photos, and collage art.

Add to that a number of sports organizations, including a few Major League Baseball teams such as the Chicago Cubs, Los Angeles Dodgers and New York Yankees, all of which have had special days for their Babe Ruth, in-stadium bobblehead giveaways. Some of the other companies in the sports arena making headway of Babe Ruth are these ones:

Forever Collectibles. Bobbleheads.

Leaf Trading Cards. Babe Ruth-themed trading card sets.

Topps. Trading cards and packaging rights.

Panini. Trading cards and packaging rights.

Winning Streak Sports. Wool pennants and banners.

Hall of Fame Games. Babe Ruth-themed board game.

The list goes on and on.

The Donruss Company is a manufacturer of sports cards that was founded in 1954 and acquired by the Panini Group in 2009. But back in 2003 Donruss purchased a 1925 jersey that Babe Ruth had worn for the New York Yankees. It was one of only three known Ruth game-worn jerseys which made it a very rare commodity. The company had paid $264,210 for the jersey at an auction and then did what some pundits thought sacrilege; they brought in Ruth's daughter Julia, then a spry eighty-six-year-old, along with her son Tom, and staged a ceremonial *cutting* of the jersey. Donruss later had the jersey cut into 2,100 pieces, swatches to be imbedded in a new series of high-end, collectible trading cards — 2,100 memorabilia trading cards in all. The company created ninety-five copies of the card and sold them for $2,500 each which netted an immediate return of $237,500 for that one product alone.

Julia Ruth Stevens, Tom Stevens, and Hall of Famer Gary Carter with the 1925 Babe Ruth jersey which was cut into swatches.

Julia wearing the jersey before the cutting.

"It was close to what we had paid for the jersey," says Ben Ecklar, Director of Product Development for Baseball at Panini America, which is the biggest manufacturer of sports collectibles in the world.

Over the years Donruss, and later Panini, has created some 2,263 cards that feature Babe Ruth and the 1925 New York Yankees pinstripe jersey. These cards have been inserted into packs of cards across a number of brands and product releases. Ecklar says having Babe Ruth in those products creates brand awareness for the company, and that Ruth himself and the jersey create not only content but also excellent value for all these programs.

Ecklar, who had worked with Donruss as early as 2001 and who has been doing Babe Ruth deals since that time, had a photograph of himself taken wearing the Ruth jersey. In fact, many employees of the company had their photo taken with the jersey.

The Babe Ruth 1936 Hall of Fame card includes pieces of
Ruth's bat, his pants and his Yankees road jersey from
the 1925 season. Value of the card is $1,000.

"It was a lot of money for a jersey at the time," he says, "but today
that jersey would be worth ten times that amount. We did it to create
some really cool trading cards featuring swatches of the jersey so you
could actually touch a piece of the jersey in the card. Babe Ruth is the
marquis name in our baseball product. From an iconic standpoint he
was the dominant American icon. Any chance to have Babe Ruth in
our card set is good for us and good for the hobby."

By the *hobby*, Ecklar means the business, the industry, right down
to the individual collector, and he says Ruth is the one every collector
wants. Indeed, Ecklar acknowledges that current baseball stars might
be prominent among card collectors and will remain so as long as they
keep hitting home runs. But he says Ruth is in a class of his own.

"He is the constant standard and he was bigger than baseball.
Individual market sales for Babe Ruth are higher than for anybody
else. You have Lou Gehrig. Jackie Robinson. Ty Cobb. Joe DiMaggio.
Mickey Mantle. They're all big but they're all secondary to Ruth."

Why? Ecklar offers his own take.

"Ever since I was a kid he's been *the* household name. He put the New York Yankees on the stage. He put baseball on the stage. When you talk about passion for baseball and the history of baseball he is the pioneer. And he has always been beyond sports. Everybody wants a piece of Babe Ruth."

A relative newcomer to the Ruth fold is Norwegian, a European airline which is rapidly expanding around the world, including in the United States. For many years, beginning in 2002, the airline has been celebrating iconic, historical figures from such fields as art, literature, music and entertainment, and sports. It puts the faces of these *heroes* on the tail fins of its jets and started with noteworthy Scandinavians such as Norwegian painter Edvard Munch who is best known for his painting *The Scream*. Then the airline expanded the idea to other nationalities as its route network became global — such people as aviation pioneer Sir Freddie Laker and author Jonathan Swift, for example. It is a marketing concept that literally gives a human face to an airline. Norwegian has now expanded its Tailfin Heroes program to celebrate its U.S. routes.

Who was the first American it selected?

"Babe Ruth is our first American on a Boeing 787 Dreamliner aircraft," says Thomas Ramdahl, Chief Commercial Officer at Norwegian. "We have a few other Americans flying on our smaller 737 MAX 8 aircraft fleet. They include Sojourner Truth [African-American abolitionist and activist for women's rights who died in 1883], Clara Barton [Civil War nurse who founded the American Red Cross], and Benjamin Franklin [one of the Founding Fathers of the United States]."

Why Babe Ruth?

"There is nothing more American than baseball," says Ramdahl, "and the Bambino set record after record, helping shape the sport into the national and worldwide spectacle that it is today. In a time when so much divides us, the sport of baseball is one rare pastime that brings people together. The game Babe Ruth devoted his life to

was, and still is, part of the glue that forms the fabric of the United States, which makes him a perfect choice. He has inspired so many millions of people, and this is our homage to him."

Ramdahl then shares a quote he got from the Leigh Montville biography *The Big Bam: The Life and Times of Babe Ruth* (Random House, 2006): "If sport has become the national religion, Babe Ruth is the patron saint."

Norwegian has a page on its website dedicated to *tailfin heroes* where it says: 'It felt only natural for us to adorn the tails of our aircraft with personalities who have pushed the boundaries, challenged the established and inspired others.'

So what began as a Norwegian affair soon became international. After all, the airline is global, and so is Babe Ruth.

But that is only the private sector. On July 6, 1983 the United States Postal Service issued its first Babe Ruth stamp — a twenty-cent stamp issued in conjunction with the 50th anniversary of baseball's first All-Star Game. Alas, it was none other than Ruth who hit the very first All-Star Game home run at that 1933 affair. How many of those stamps were issued a half century later? A lot — 184,950,000 to be exact — or *not quite two hundred million*. Put another way, it was almost one stamp for every single American.

Collecting a few of those stamps would have been a good investment. In 2013 the Mystic Stamp Company was listing those twenty-cent stamps for $1.25 new or twenty-five cents used. And then on May 25, 1998, yet another Babe Ruth stamp made its appearance — this time a thirty-two-cent stamp — which was issued as part of a commemorative series to celebrate the Roaring Twenties. Not many people have appeared on more than one U.S. stamp, but there is another ballplayer. Roberto Clemente, a star outfielder, was a native of Puerto Rico who was deeply involved in charity work throughout Latin America and the Caribbean. On December 31, 1972, he was on a mission delivering aid to earthquake victims in Nicaragua when his plane went down. He was only thirty-eight. Clemente also has two stamps.

"Champions get many a small boy to eat a good breakfast!"

In the 1920s and 1930s Babe Ruth was in a class by himself as a celebrity who endorsed products. He lent his name to cars, hats, coats, underwear, cigarettes, cereal, Girl Guide Cookies, soap, what have you. No surprise but *Wheaties* and the 'breakfast of champions' once put him on a cereal box with a star-struck boy looking up at him.

In 1921 — some pundits say that was the best year of his career — Ruth was enjoying his second season with the Yankees and managed to slug fifty-nine home runs which was a new record. The year before, in 1920, he had hit fifty-four and in the process obliterated the previous mark of twenty-nine which he had set himself as a member of the Boston Red Sox. That was in 1919, the first year he was a full-time hitter. So every year the same guy keeps breaking his own home-run record. He was also routinely out-homering entire *teams*. Add to the mix the fact all this was happening in the wake of the ugly Black Sox Scandal, and so, the masses were rushing to see him and Ruth became the widely acclaimed savior of baseball. He wasn't only the toast of Broadway, but the toast of America itself.

In the fall of 1921 he had established himself as baseball's all-time, home-run king, supplanting Roger Connor and his lifetime total of 138 which had been garnered between 1880 and 1897.

Enter the Baby Ruth Candy Bar.

Ruth's name was magic everywhere. He was at the very top of the baseball world, but at the bottom was the moribund Chicago Cubs of the National League. Not far from their home at Wrigley Field was the headquarters of the Curtiss Candy Company. The company had an item called the Kandy Kake, which like the Cubs wasn't doing that well. Then they changed the recipe and came up with a catchy new name — the Baby Ruth.

Sales promptly went through the roof and by 1926 the Baby Ruth Candy Bar was doing $1 million a month which was pretty heady for those days. In the process the Curtiss Candy Company became the world's no. 1 candy maker.

That same year, 1926, Ruth licensed his name to the George H. Ruth Candy Company and tried to get a patent for Ruth's Home Run Candy. The Curtiss Candy Company, which already had a runaway best-seller with its Baby Ruth Candy Bar, sued for copyright infringement. What's more, the company said its candy bar had nothing to do with the baseball star, but had been named after the oldest daughter of President Grover Cleveland, a girl whose first name happened to be Ruth. Never mind that Ruth Cleveland had died back in 1904.

In 1931 a patent court ruled in favor of Curtiss. Then, in 1933 — one year after Ruth's celebrated Called Shot Home Run in the 1932 World Series — Curtiss erected an illuminated sign for the Baby Ruth Candy Bar high on a rooftop. It could be seen just beyond the center-field wall at Wrigley Field.

Home runs? Baseball? The Baby Ruth Candy Bar?

The sign stood in that spot for forty years even though Babe Ruth had nothing to do with the candy bar.

Fast-forward to 1995 and the year of the Ruth centennial. The company representing the Ruth estate, which at the time was CMG, licensed his name and likeness for use in a Baby Ruth marketing campaign. Finally, it seemed justice was being done. But from 1926 to 1995 neither Babe Ruth nor any member of his family ever made a cent from the Baby Ruth Candy Bar.

The Curtiss Candy Company was sold in 1963 and eventually wound up in the hands of Nestlé which today is one of many companies that has associated itself with Babe Ruth.

On the surface the story about the Baby Ruth candy bar might sound as if Curtiss the candy maker had succeeded in preventing Ruth and his heirs from profiting in a product that benefited from the perceived connection. This is the kind of thing that involves a company like the Luminary Group. It protects the name, image and other intellectual property of those deceased celebrities, and that means working closely with the families of those celebrities. In this case that means the Ruth estate, which consists of the surviving family members of Babe Ruth, and the Babe Ruth League. Luminary Group works closely with the Ruth estate in policing the marketplace for unauthorized uses, while also proactively searching for appropriate advertising, promotional and merchandise opportunities. With every merchandising deal signed, royalties are paid to the estate on items sold.

As with any business, there are always upturns and downturns, and the licensing of deceased celebrities is no different. However, according to Pete Enfield of the Luminary Group, Babe Ruth is a valuable brand that continues to generate recognition. Says Enfield: "He was an overwhelmingly positive figure, and from a licensing perspective for a sports legend, he is at the very top. Babe transcends baseball. He is an icon who is recognized beyond his sport and now, seventy years after his death, his licensing activity is as vibrant as it's been anytime in the past thirty years. He has not only survived, but he has thrived."

Enfield says people will still be talking about Ruth twenty, thirty and fifty years from now, and they will be talking about him in the same regard that we talk about him today. In short, Babe Ruth stands the test of time.

"There is a lot of safety and security in associating with an iconic personality like Babe Ruth," says Enfield. "In addition to his record-breaking career, he had such a strong and deep connection with his fans, and kids in particular, which is one of the many reasons why his appeal has endured for so many decades."

But back to that Baby Ruth Candy Bar which has seen a lot of action over the years. It has been featured in movies — *Caddyshack* (1980), *The Goonies* (1985), *The Mighty* (1998), *Hellboy* (2004), and once — many years before any of those movies — it even made it into the title of a film, namely, *A Rose and a Baby Ruth* (1956).

Then there is the all-time favorite baseball movie of Julia Ruth Stevens — *The Sandlot* — which was made in 1993. It is a tender story about a group of boys who play sandlot baseball, but Scotty Smalls, the new kid in town, has never played the game and knows nothing about it. Nothing. But he does have a baseball, courtesy of his father, and that ball had been signed by Babe Ruth. When Scotty brings the ball to a game and it gets slugged over the fence, apparently lost, he tells the other boys that the ball had been signed by a woman. Some woman named *Baby Ruth*. The dialogue that follows — the screenplay was written by David Mickey Evans and Robert Gunter — between Smalls and the boys is telling about the universal appeal and persona of Babe Ruth.

Says Timmy: "Smalls, you mean to tell me that you went home and swiped a ball ... that was signed by Babe Ruth, and you brought it here and actually played with it? Actually played with it?"

"Yeah," replies Smalls, "but I was gonna bring it back."

"But it was signed by Babe Ruth."

"Yeah. Yeah. Yeah. You keep telling me that. Who is she?"

With that Timmy is nothing short of incredulous.

"What? What?" he says.

Sacrilege. Then the other boys join in, one by one.

"The Sultan of Swat. The King of Crash. The Colossus of Clout. The Colossus of Clout."

And then altogether.

"Babe Ruth! The great Bambino!"

"Oh, my God!" says Smalls. "That's the same guy?"

"Yeah Smalls," says another boy. "Babe Ruth is the greatest baseball player that ever lived. People say he was less than a God but more than a man. Ya know, like Hercules or somethin'."[31]

Hercules indeed. Enfield says Babe Ruth generates significant income to the estate every year and this has been going on for a long time. He singles out the trading card companies as valuable licensing partners.

"The trading card companies, Topps and Panini in particular, have been great licensees of the estate for many years as they produce high-quality product, highlight his remarkable records and accomplishments, and continue to introduce Babe to younger generations," he says. "They pay market-leading, annual licensing fees to the estate for the right to feature Babe on their products which has been a win-win for both sides. The advertising deals are also significant revenue generators for the estate as these regional and national campaigns often result in a premium, one-time fee. Additionally, the estate has several long-time merchandise licensees that play an incredibly valuable role in the Babe Ruth licensing program, and they continue to work closely with the estate in developing new artwork and designs that are fresh, exciting and relevant to current consumer demands. These successful programs generate a consistent, annual income stream for the estate."

Babe Ruth being what he is — *present tense* — Enfield says the Luminary Group and the estate are selective in any merchandise deals they grant.

"We first look for partners that will maintain and enhance the Babe Ruth brand in a positive manner. Once that is established, we then assess the company's strategy for Babe. Each deal the estate enters into, big or small, is a valuable component to the overall licensing program. That said, in today's climate, a particular focus is placed on working with companies whose merchandise programs have legs. By that I mean we are not looking for programs that last just a short period of time. Our goal is to enter into multi-year collaborations with companies who are in it for the long haul."

Babe Ruth, like that Hercules character, is forever lasting.

*"Babe Ruth is king of the whole business
of sports memorabilia. He is in so much demand that
I could make a living just out of Babe Ruth items."*
— David Kohler, President, SCP Auctions

Chapter 8

BUSINESS, BUCKS AND THE BABE

This Babe Ruth-signed baseball from 1927 sold
at auction for a record $388,375 in 2012

LEGENDARY BROADCASTER Vin Scully, who retired in 2016, could always be counted on for a good yarn when he was calling Los Angeles Dodgers games and September 9, 2014 was no exception. It just happened to be Babe Ruth Bobblehead Day at Dodgers Stadium. Never mind that Ruth never played for the Dodgers and his only connection with the team was in 1938, three years after his retirement, when he was hired as the first-base coach for the then Brooklyn Dodgers. During the broadcast that day Scully, who was born in 1927, told his listeners about the time when he was a kid and had met Ruth in the flesh at the Polo Grounds in New York.

He said there was a big commotion in the upper deck in right field so he went to see what it was all about and there was Babe Ruth in a cap and camel hair coat, surrounded by kids clamoring for his autograph. Scully said Ruth reached into his side pocket and took out a stack of business cards. On one side they were blank and on the other side was a stamped Babe Ruth signature. The great Bambino promptly handed out the cards.

Scully said he got one for himself, but figured it wouldn't be worth much these days because it wasn't a real signature. It was just a stamp. Still, it was in the same beautifully handwritten signature Ruth had always been known for. However, if Ruth had signed that card with his own hand things would be different.

In 2012 a baseball he had signed from the 1927 season fetched the princely sum of $388,375 at an auction held at the 33rd Annual National Sports Collectors Convention in Baltimore. The ball had once been owned by none other than Ted Williams. The buyer was Jeff Rosenberg, president of TRISTAR Productions, Inc., which is a collector of high-end sports memorabilia. Rosenberg called the ball "the Mona Lisa of autographed baseballs."

Seven years earlier — on August 17, 2005 — the same Rosenberg had been interviewed by *The Houston Chronicle* for a story about sports collecting and its long-term prospects. In the article he said his company's sports business had grown every year, he expected it to keep growing, and he was "bullish" on the industry. He also added this: "Ten years ago a Babe Ruth jersey sold for $10,000. One just sold for over $900,000."[32]

That interview was conducted in 2005, but fast-forward to the same year Rosenberg bought that baseball in 2012. That was the year another Babe Ruth jersey would sell for a world-record price of over $4.4 million.

In 1915 Col. Jacob Ruppert and Captain Tillinghast L'Hommedieu Huston purchased the New York Yankees baseball team for $1.25 million. In 2017, just over a hundred years later, *Forbes* pegged the value of the franchise at $3.7 billion.[33] By any stretch, even for that length of time, this is remarkable growth. If we keep the time frame at an even century and do the math, it would mean that during those hundred years the value of the New York Yankees rose at an annual rate of about 29.6% which is a much better rate of return than the stock market. During the 20th century the stock market grew at an average rate of 10.4% a year.[34] So, as a pure investment vehicle, the Yankees performed about three times as well as the stock market. Of course, a good chunk of that growth — in the 1920s and 1930s — was largely due to one player.

Babe Ruth.

In 2012 his Yankees jersey circa 1920 sold at auction for exactly $4,415,658. The 1920 season was Ruth's first on Broadway and he made the most of it — a .376 batting average, fifty-four home runs which demolished his previous record of twenty-nine, and 137 runs batted in. But what might be of more fascination from the purely financial side of things is that attendance for New York Yankees games at the Polo Grounds in the 1920 season *doubled* from the previous year to 1.29 million people.

All because of him.

What was Ruth's Yankees jersey worth back in the early '20s? If it had a value of $100 — and sold for over $4.4 million a century later — then the average annual rate of return over the next hundred years would have been about 440%. *Per year.* If it had a value of $1,000 in the early '20s — that would have been an unfathomable sum of money for a baseball jersey at the time — the average rate of annual return over the next century would still have been about 44%. *Per year.* No matter how you look at it, over the last one hundred years, that Babe Ruth jersey would have been a better long-term investment than the New York Yankees and a much better long-term investment than the stock market.

The question is *why*.

Consider his autograph. His name is on pretty well any list concerning the most valuable signatures and if it's strictly a baseball list then it's no contest. One website featuring the Top 20 Baseball Autographs in the Hobby put him at no. 1 with this kicker:

> Babe Ruth's autograph is, quite simply, the most desired in the
> hobby. Luckily for contemporary fans, Ruth was, perhaps, the most
> prolific signer of his era. Nevertheless, the zeal for items signed
> by the Sultan of Swat has not wavered in nearly 80 years, leaving
> demand to outweigh supply.[35]

Go beyond baseball and the world of sports and he is still up there. A website called *10 of the World's Most Expensive Autographs* had that 1927 Babe Ruth-autographed baseball at no. 4. That put Ruth ahead of a contract signed by Jimmy Hendrix, a baseball signed by Joe DiMaggio and Marilyn Monroe, a photograph of Albert Einstein signed by the great man himself, a guitar signed by musician Jimmy Page, the only known photograph to be signed by outlaw Jesse James, and a copy of *The Dallas Morning News* from November 22, 1963 that was signed by John. F. Kennedy a mere two hours before his assassination.[36]

What about the three signatures ahead of Ruth on that list? Even this is telling. No. 3 was the Double Fantasy album signed by John

Lennon to his killer Mark Chapman on the very day of Lennon's murder. No. 2 was the Emancipation Proclamation signed by Abraham Lincoln. And no. 1 was the Acts of Congress — George Washington's personal copy of the Constitution, Bill of Rights, and the First Congress — signed by Washington himself.

And that was it, so Ruth is in good company. But when it comes to the business of sports memorabilia, he is in a class by himself.

In January, 2016 a listing of the fifteen most valuable pieces of sports memorabilia ever sold — for any sport in the world, anywhere in the world — included no fewer than *seven items* involving Babe Ruth.

No. 1 was the Yankees jersey that fetched the $4.4 million plus. No. 2, and the record-holder until the Ruth jersey sold in 2012, was the original hand-written rules of basketball by the sport's inventor, James Naismith. Another item on the list was the hockey jersey worn by Canada's Paul Henderson from the 1972 Canada-Soviet Summit Series. Two items were from soccer — the Sheffield Football Club Rules, Regulations and Laws, dating from 1857, and the FA (Football Association) Challenge Cup from 1997. There was one item from boxing — the gloves Muhammad Ali wore in his 1965 heavyweight title fight against Floyd Patterson.

The other ten on the top-fifteen list were all from baseball, such is the high profile of the sport in the business of sports collectibles. There was the ball hit by Mark McGwire for his 70th home run in 1998, a Honus Wagner baseball card from 1909, and the ball hit by Henry Aaron for his 755th home run in 1974, which left seven other things from baseball — and all seven of them had to do with Babe Ruth. In addition to the world-record, $4.4-million jersey, the other six were:

- Ruth's Yankees jersey from 1933 — sold for $657,250.

- his uniform from the 1934 World Tour which took the American League All-Stars to Japan — sold for $771,000 and later sold privately for $1.65 million.

- a home run ball he signed from the 1933 all-star game — sold for $805,000.

- his Yankees jersey from 1932 — sold for $940,000.

- his 1919 contract with the Yankees — sold for $996,000.

- the bat he used to hit the very first home run at Yankee Stadium in 1923 — sold for $1.265 million.[37]

Sports memorabilia is an ever-evolving industry with new records being set all the time in various categories. An online auction that wound up on June 30, 2017 pushed a couple other Ruth items onto that list, too, both of them sold by actor Charlie Sheen, who is a long-time Ruth aficionado. There was the actual contract by which Ruth was traded from the Red Sox to the Yankees in 1920 which sold for $2.3 million; Sheen had bought it in the 1990s for $150,000. The other item was Ruth's 1927 World Series ring which sold for $2.1 million. Sheen had also bought that in the 1990s and had paid $225,000.

Not a bad rate of return.

Ruth being what he is, many other Ruth items are also up there, such as his 1914 rookie card which once sold at auction for just under half a million dollars. That sale happened in 2013 and the card was even rated poor quality.

The National Sports Collectors Convention where Jeff Rosenberg bought that Babe Ruth baseball for $388,375 is an annual trade show for sports memorabilia. It was first held in 1980 in Los Angeles and, at the time, had been pretty well confined to collectors of sports cards. But since then the industry has grown by leaps and bounds. A typical convention features hundreds of dealer booths and athletes who are on hand to sign celebrity autographs. How big is the convention? That largely depends on where it is held, but the 1991 convention in Anaheim, California was the first one to attract over 100,000 attendees.

It is big business and it's all business. Hypothesize for a moment and imagine that Babe Ruth was alive today. No doubt, he would be asked to sign baseball cards at one of these conventions, and the organizers would want to charge collectors and fans for every autograph he provided. For him that autograph would command a great deal of money, certainly more than for any other player. A few years ago the great Willie Mays was signing at the convention and prices for his autographed baseball started at $300 a pop, rising to $800 for a signed bat. The only problem is that Ruth signed his name to more bats, balls, caps, what have you, than any baseball player or any other athlete alive or dead — and never charged a cent — unless it was for a charity.

Chances are good that Ruth would have told the organizers to go jump. Indeed, he might have insisted that no kid be turned away and he would sign at no charge.

The history of the sports collectibles industry, and especially baseball, had its roots in the 19th century. In the latter half of that century baseball was getting more and more popular. In fact, the earliest known baseball card is a team card from 1860 which means it pre-dates the Civil War. The Brooklyn Atlantics card had been in the same family for over 150 years and was sold through Heritage Auctions in Chicago in 2015 for $179,250. But it was the tobacco industry that really got things going with sports cards.

In 1887 Goodwin & Company, a New York tobacco manufacturer, was credited with being the first to produce tobacco trading cards featuring baseball players. The company also made cards with boxers and other celebrities. But these cards from 1887 were considered the first collectibles. Another early player in the business was the Old Judge Tobacco Company with its 'Photographs of all the professional base ball players, celebrated pugilists and leading actresses.'[38]

The name Honus Wagner is legendary in the card business and with him it was also the tobacco companies that produced his baseball cards, but Wagner was a bit of an anomaly, especially for that time, because he objected to being associated with tobacco. Soon his card was pulled which is why so few of them are in existence and why they are so valuable. Wagner's celeb rated T206 card produced by the American Tobacco Company is often recognized as the most valuable sports card ever.

In 1986 it sold for $25,000. In 1991 it was purchased by hockey great Wayne Gretzky and Bruce McNall, then owner of the NHL's Los Angeles Kings, for $451,000. Four years later it sold for $500,000 and in 2007 it sold for $2.8 million. How much it is worth now is anyone's guess. However, the Babe Ruth rookie card from 1914 when he was a minor-pro AAA player is also pretty rare. If such a card exists today in pristine condition, and no such commodity has ever surfaced, experts say it could fetch *$5 million.*

Maybe more.

In the 1930s bubble gum companies got into the act in a big way and in 1952 Topps released what was the first baseball card to feature the image of a player, along with his team's logo, player information, and his individual stats. And things have grown from there. In the 1980s something else happened as pro sports teams started to sell

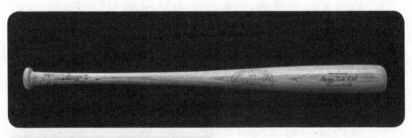

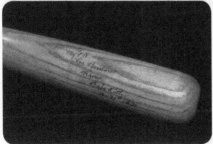

Babe Ruth gave this signed bat to Lou Breslow, a writer and director who worked with him on a series of short films called *Play Ball with Babe Ruth*, which were released in 1932. In 2017 it sold for $317,250

their team jerseys in stores directly to the public. Then came the online world. All this goes into the mix, but the one constant in the industry that is ever changing and ever growing is that Babe Ruth remains solidly entrenched at no. 1.

David Kohler is a big player in the business who got into the sports collectibles industry by accident. He had planned to go into medicine. After studying premed at the University of California, Irvine, he went to California State University, Fullerton, and when not in class he could be found running a small sports shop. Things went so well for him that he decided to abandon his medical career and concentrate on collecting and the auction side of the sports memorabilia business. Today SCP Auctions, which was founded by Kohler in 1979, is one of the biggest auctioneers and private sellers of sports memorabilia and cards. SCP has even partnered with the prestigious Sotheby's for the auction of high-end items.

SCP can attach its name to a long list of sports memorabilia that have fetched record and near-record prices:

1. Babe Ruth Yankees jersey, circa 1920 — $4.415 million

2. 1857 'Laws of Base Ball' three-document set — $3.263 million

3. 1936 Olympics gold medal won by Jesse Owens in Berlin — $1.47 million

4. signed Babe Ruth bat for first home run hit at Yankee Stadium in 1923 — $1.265 million

5. contract selling Babe Ruth from the Red Sox to the Yankees — $996,000

6. ball hit by Barry Bonds for his 756th home run breaking Henry Aaron's record — $752,467

7. gold pocket watch presented to Babe Ruth by the Yankees during his last visit to Yankee Stadium — $650,108

8. bat used by Kirk Gibson to hit game-winning home run in Game 1 of 1988 World Series — $575,912

9. Yankee cap worn by Babe Ruth from the 1930s — $537,278.

So, once again, Ruth dominates as he is involved with no fewer than *five* of those top nine sales. We can also add in the two sales made by actor Charlie Sheen in 2017 when he sold Ruth's 1927 World Series ring, and the contract that brought Ruth from the Red Sox to the Yankees. That contract comes embellished with a significant back-story, namely, the celebrated Curse of the Bambino which set the Red Sox off on nearly a century of oblivion — eighty-six years to be exact — before they would win another World Series. During the same time frame the Yankees would win some twenty-six World Series titles, the first four with Ruth at the helm.

Sheen had bought the contract for $150,000 in the 1990s and wound up selling it for $2.3 million. Said auctioneer Lelands prior to the sale: "This is ... akin to some of the great documents in the history of our country. The Declaration of Independence, Lincoln's Draft of the Gettysburg Address or Albert Einstein's 'Theory of Relativity' Papers."

As for Ruth's World Series ring from 1927, that was special, too, because the Yankees of that season were and still are regarded as the best baseball team in history. Sheen had bought the ring for $225,000 and in the 2017 auction it went for $2.1 million, a new record for a sports ring.

SCP's David Kohler candidly says that Ruth is the *king* of the sports memorabilia business, that when it comes to individuals there is a big drop-off after him, and that no. 2 is up for grabs. He says Ruth is unquestionably the *litmus test* for an item. That means if a Ruth bat is worth such-and-such, then a bat signed by Lou Gehrig would be based on what the Ruth bat sold for, and right on down the list. In that sense Babe Ruth is akin to the U.S. dollar as far as world currencies are concerned. He is the measuring stick, the standard, or as Kohler likes to say, "the top of the Dow Jones index."

Kohler gets no argument from Joe Orlando who runs Professional Sports Authenticator (PSA), which is considered the leading player in third-party authentication and grading services for high-value collectibles such as trading cards, tickets, packs, autographs and memorabilia. PSA is neither a collector nor a buyer. It is effectively an impartial, third-party service that offers a professional opinion about authenticity and quality. Take any annual National Sports Collectors Convention and PSA is the single biggest exhibitor at the show. It authenticates more than 150,000 items every month and over the years has authenticated about thirty million items in all.

Thirty million.

Says Orlando: "If somebody said to me, Joe, we'll give you a million dollars and you must spend it in the collectibles world, I can't think of a more stable investment than Babe Ruth. All you have to do is check with the auction houses over the last three decades. Babe Ruth set the standard and it'll never be eclipsed. He has set the standard in every single category of memorabilia."

PSA has been in the business since 1991. Prior to that time the then-fledgling industry was having a big problem with fraud. Fraud is still a concern, but now it is much tougher for a fraudulent item

 to get through the approval and authentication process. Orlando points out that with Babe Ruth autographs the 'rejection rate' still approaches 50% and more. Even today. He explains that in Ruth's latter years, when he was suffering from ill health, his night nurse would recreate his signature for the countless requests for his autograph. There was no malice intended, it was merely to satisfy the huge appetite from the public, but in the 1980s many of those autographs went undetected as real Babe Ruth originals.

Joe Orlando of PSA

Orlando says that when it comes to the business it really boils down to this: "There is Babe Ruth, then there is everyone else." He offers his own assessment as to why Ruth is supreme. "He represented the American dream. Rags to riches. Babe Ruth is the ultimate example of someone who came from nothing and became the most famous human being in the United States."

This, he says, even goes beyond what Ruth did on the baseball diamond and what he did on the diamond, Orlando adds, has never been equalled.

"They talk about the big home run hitters today. But Babe Ruth out-homered teams! And he did that routinely. Take the best left-handed pitcher today and combine him with the best hitter in baseball and that is what Babe Ruth was. There has never been anyone like him."

Kevin Keating, a top expert in autograph authentication with PSA, has forty-five years of experience in collecting — going back to when he was a boy — and more than twenty years of experience as a dealer and authenticator in the industry. He says he has personally seen thousands and maybe tens of thousands of items signed by Babe Ruth. Never mind bats and baseballs, Keating says Ruth signed everything from newspapers, postcards, matchboxes, letters and legal documents to hot dog wrappers, ping pong paddles, train schedules, hotel stationery, you name it. The list even includes bowling shoes and a dumbbell. Keating figures that during his heyday Ruth signed his signature some two million times! How is that possible? Keating said he was arguably the most famous personality in the country from 1920 to 1948 and couldn't go *anywhere* without entire towns knowing that he was present.

Keating does the math. Two million signatures over that time frame translates to 196 signatures a day which he doesn't think is out of line.

"Everywhere he went people clamored for his autograph," he says, "and as stories have it he always obliged. And even without associated monetary value to his signature during his lifetime, people valued his autograph enough to keep it as a family heirloom. One more thing

— he answered his mail which came in when he was and wasn't in town. It was a constant and he always answered up until 1947 when a ghost-signer started answering 'some' of the autograph requests. He didn't get time off from signing demands. They were omnipresent and he was gracious in meeting the demands on him."

According to Keating, it is reasonable to assume that half of all the signatures Ruth signed have been lost or destroyed over the years, which still leaves one million autographs out there. If that is true, it represents a great deal of money.

At least one of those signatures is reputedly on a baseball inside the cornerstone of Bloomingdale's department store at Lexington Avenue and 59th Street in Manhattan. The cornerstone, laid in 1930, contained a time capsule. The time capsule, not to be opened until two hundred years had passed — that would be the year 2130 — is said to include a horseshoe, a radio set, a wedding ring, a cocktail shaker, predictions of the future as written by prominent Americans, a golf ball signed by the legendary Bobby Jones, and a baseball signed by Babe Ruth. Ruth is also alleged to be one of those 'prominent Americans' who predicted the future, the others being President Calvin Coolidge who had left office one year earlier, automaker Henry Ford, and Broadway impresario Florenz Ziegfeld who was best known for his Ziegfeld Follies.

When this first got reported in the press on August 21, 2017, *The New York Times* interviewed Leila Dunbar who is an appraiser of sports memorabilia. She said the Bobby Jones-signed golf ball would be very rare and might be worth as much as $100,000. Jones won golf's Grand Slam in 1930 and was an anomaly; he was a lawyer who had played golf as an amateur but often beat the best pros of the day. He also helped design the Augusta National Golf Club and co-founded the Masters Tournament. Jones, who died in 1971, was and remains a monumental figure in the world of golf.

But Dunbar said the Babe Ruth-signed baseball would fetch $500,000 at auction — or five times what the Bobby Jones golf ball would get.

This 1918 contract signed by Babe Ruth
sold for $1,028,500 in 2014.

"He [Ruth] was probably the best known person in America," she said.

Another person who knows a lot about sports memorabilia is Ray Schulte. Back in the 1980s he worked with advertising company J. Walter Thompson in New York City and then decided to start his own sports marketing management agency. One of his early clients was baseball player Don Mattingly of the Yankees. Soon Schulte was doing consulting for several corporate clients, including Major League Baseball, the NFL, NHL, and NBA. Working with league licensees and sports memorabilia companies became a big part of his business, especially where it concerned signature authenticity and product licensing. Eventually Schulte was asked to oversee the annual National Sports Collectors Convention as its Director of Media and Public Relations.

Today Schulte Sports Marketing & Public Relations, Inc. represents athletes from a wide range of sports. It handles everything from marketing and public relations to endorsements and athlete appearances. In short, Schulte is a man who knows the business inside out.

What are the main components that determine the price of an item in the world of sports memorabilia? According to Schulte, the value of a piece of sports memorabilia is generally relative to the profile of the piece itself and is primarily determined by the demand relative to the supply. But other factors come into play as well — authenticity, condition, degree of provenance which refers to the item's place of origin or its earliest known history, as well as grading, appraisal value, and *the popularity of the athlete or sport.*

Says Schulte: "Babe Ruth items are in constant demand, so when you see auction houses posting Babe Ruth game-used bats, signed baseballs, photos, vintage trading cards, and personal items such as the gold pocket watch the New York Yankees presented to him, collectors take notice. And Babe Ruth collectible and memorabilia items will always be in demand. He has become a great investment and cherished memory for many collectors and sports enthusiasts both at home and throughout the world. He is universally recognized as the 'Sultan of Swat' and not only on the field, but also for what he did off the field."

Schulte uses a word that many other people use when talking about Babe Ruth. He says Ruth *transcended* baseball.

"He was and still is bigger than life. He was beloved because he was the New York Yankees slugger and won multiple world championships, but many people were also attracted to his bigger-than-life personality. He played golf, hunted, fished, visited children's hospitals, entertained politicians, and played Santa Claus for the under-privileged. And the media loved him."

Schulte first met Julia Ruth Stevens outside Yankee Stadium in 1990 and immediately became friends with her. He also admits that he himself is a big Babe Ruth fan, and why not?

"He was the guy who made it all happen for us."

The thing with Babe Ruth is that he is at the top when it comes to sheer numbers — numbers concerning just about anything that can be measured — but some things are hard to measure, such as the popularity or likeability quotient of an athlete, or of any person for that matter.

Indeed, mention Babe Ruth and the value his name brings, and other names that crop up tend to be Abraham Lincoln, George Washington or Albert Einstein, but then no one ever sold an article of clothing worn by any of those men for $4.4 million. And that, of course, would be *the jersey* — Ruth's game-worn New York Yankees jersey circa 1920— that would fetch a world-record price sixty-four years after his death. Such is the enduring power and magnitude of Babe Ruth.

"If Babe Ruth touches something it turns to gold."
— *Mike Heffner, co-owner of Lelands*

Chapter 9

THE

WORLD-RECORD

JERSEY

THE MYSTERY BUYER would be represented by Lelands, an auction house that specializes in 'Sports and Americana Memorabilia, Vintage Photography and Rock'n Roll'. On its website Lelands calls itself "the largest and most respected Sports Auction House in the world" and over the years it has sold tens of millions of dollars of vintage sports memorabilia and cards.

Only Lelands would know the identity of this Mystery Buyer, but Lelands wasn't running this particular auction. That would be another company — SCP Auctions — which back in May, 2012 was about to begin its Premier Internet Auction, one of two big online auctions it holds every year. SCP had started up in 1979 as an auctioneer and private seller of sports memorabilia and cards, and had dealt in some fascinating items.

There was the T206 Honus Wagner tobacco card issued from 1909 to 1911 for the famous baseball player who was known as The Flying Dutchman. Wagner, widely considered one of the greatest players in history, won eight National League batting titles during his illustrious career. In 2007 the card fetched $2.8 million.

There was the ball hit by Barry Bonds when he smashed his 756th home run to break Henry Aaron's all-time record. In that same year, 2007, the ball sold for $752,467. But the estimated value of that ball has since been watered down due to the steroid scandal, which has plagued baseball and has absorbed Bonds and other sluggers, not to mention the fact that Bonds was never much of a fan favorite anyway.

All these ingredients go into the financial mixer to determine the worth of an item.

The Bob Cousy collection of basketball memorabilia was also sold at an SCP auction. Cousy, who led the Boston Celtics to eleven championships in the 1950s and 1960s, had compiled a collection of personal effects during his storied career. The stockpile included his 1952 NBA All-Star uniform, his 1957 MVP trophy, a photograph signed to him by none other than John F. Kennedy, and a host of other things. The whole slew sold in 2003 for $455,000.

SCP's Premier Internet Auction in May, 2012 would be special, and Lelands and its Mystery Buyer were ready. One of the items up for grabs was a New York Yankee jersey worn by Babe Ruth in the early 1920s. The 1920 season was the legendary Bambino's first on Broadway. At the time Ruth had already become the biggest star in the game and was the holder of a new single-season home-run record as he had just slugged twenty-nine dingers for the Boston Red Sox a year earlier. But then he got traded from the Red Sox to the Yankees and the celebrated Curse of the Bambino began; Ruth himself was a member, a pitcher no less, of Red Sox World Series championship teams in 1915, 1916 and 1918, but after the trade the Red Sox wouldn't win again until 2004. As for the jersey, it was the oldest known Babe Ruth jersey in existence.

David Kohler, Founder and President of SCP Auctions, is a respected dealer of *rare sports collectibles* as these things are called. In addition to handling some very rare and pricey items, he is a founding board member of the Sports Collectibles Association International, which promotes ethics in the sports collectibles industry. He gets interviewed by the likes of *USA Today, CNN, ESPN, Sports Illustrated,* and *The New York Times* if anything truly monumental happens in the business.

David Kohler
of SCP Auctions

When the May, 2012 Premier Internet Auction was over, Kohler found himself doing a lot of interviews.

At the outset he figured the Ruth jersey might fetch $1 million and maybe even go as high as $2 million. After all, this is Babe Ruth and there are always private collectors who are willing to fork over big money — very big money — for items they want to get their hands on. Such things are not only rare, but they often appreciate in value, so it also makes good business sense. An investment if you will. At the time the most money ever fetched for a jersey had been $1,056,000 — that one had also belonged to Babe Ruth — but the deal included his pants as well.

This jersey was older than that and in very good shape.

Mike Heffner, a co-owner of Lelands, knew of five or six collectors off the top who might pay upwards of $1 million for the early-1920s Ruth jersey, and he knew one of them in particular who wanted to get his hands on this jersey real bad. *But two million dollars?* Who would pay that much? To answer that question, it is necessary to look at the jersey and its condition, the man who wore it, and also when he wore it.

Prior to the 2012 auction, the jersey had been on display for five years at the Babe Ruth Birthplace Museum in Baltimore, the city where Ruth was born in 1895. The Spalding jersey, made of wool, was a blue-grey color with 'NEW YORK' stitched in solid-blue capital letters across the front. Ballplayers didn't have their names on the jerseys in those days, but on the inside collar of this one and stitched in a fading shade of pink was *'Ruth G. H.'* Babe was a moniker that Ruth had picked up in minor-league ball; his given names were George Herman.

As with all items of sports memorabilia that go to auction, the jersey had to be evaluated for its authenticity. That was handled by a company called MEARS, which specializes in jersey grading and authentication criteria. Its experts evaluated the jersey for manufacturer characteristics such as lettering, tagging, numbering, patches, and style, and also for such things as wear and use. The jersey would then receive a rating of anywhere from A1 to A10 — A10 being the highest. MEARS wound up awarding the jersey a rating of A8. In other words, this was the real

McCoy, although after more than ninety years, not quite in pristine condition. But close.

The era of the jersey was significant, too. MEARS could not verify that it was from the 1920 season, but the chances were good. Styles of uniforms did not change from year to year back then, and there was no identification as to the particular year on the uniform. But MEARS could pinpoint the jersey to either the 1920 or 1921 season, and it is possible Ruth wore it for both seasons; indeed, major-league baseball teams were not big-ticket items in those days like they are now. And so, the era was a major factor in determining the value of the jersey, as was the man who wore it.

That would be the biggest factor of all.

In 1920 the baseball world was still reeling from the Black Sox Scandal of a year earlier when players from the American League Champion Chicago White Sox, one of the best teams in history, had taken a dive and thrown the World Series to the National League Champion Cincinnati Reds. In short, they had been paid off by gamblers. Eight members of the White Sox would soon be kicked out of the game for life. The very next season along came Babe Ruth to New York City where he single-handedly changed the game from the Ty Cobb era of hitting singles and advancing base runners inch-by-inch, in order to manufacture a run, to the big monster clout. The home run. Home runs were rare at the time, but when it did happen it was sudden and dramatic. Babe Ruth made it happen a lot and the fans loved it.

Said sportswriter Donald Honig in the 1998 ESPN documentary 'Outside the Lines: Babe Ruth's Larger Than Life Legacy: "It's almost as if when anybody hits a home run today they should pay Babe Ruth a royalty. It's like he invented it."[39]

In the 1920 season Ruth hit his fifty-four home runs, which was more than *the combined totals of every other team* in baseball except one. Needless to say, it was a new record. To put that number into perspective, consider that in the 2016 season a dozen major-league teams hit over 200 home runs while only one — the Baltimore Orioles —

hit over 250. So extrapolate what Ruth did back in 1920 and focus on the 2016 season. It would be like a modern ballplayer hitting 250 home runs *all by himself.*

Alas, the next season, 1921, Ruth did even better. He hit fifty-nine home runs.

What all this means is that the biggest name in the game was playing on the biggest stage, and the people poured through the turnstiles to watch him. In that 1920 season the Yankees became the first team in baseball history to draw more than a million fans.

As far as the jersey goes, the online attention espoused by SCP Auctions leading up to that May, 2012 Premier Internet Auction said it all. This is from their website:

> "In a time when baseball, reeling from the 1919 Black Sox scandal, declining attendance and declining credibility, needed a revitalization, Babe Ruth saved the day. By destiny's hand, the most visible, dominating, and popular athlete in American history was brought to New York City to play on baseball's biggest stage. At the dawn of the Roaring Twenties, Babe Ruth turned baseball on its head, sparking fan interest and excitement, and the birth of the most enduring dynasty in sports history."

SCP Auctions called the jersey "a national heirloom" and presented it "not merely as a piece of sports memorabilia, but as one of the most singularly important discoveries in the realm of Americana." It said: "Babe Ruth was a man of mythic proportions. More than any other athlete, he transcended sports, achieving a nearly unrivaled status as an American icon. Like the man himself, this jersey is a treasure for the ages."

So, all things considered, this Babe Ruth jersey was going to be worth a lot of money. But how much, nobody knew.

The May, 2012 Premier Internet Auction took place over twenty days — non-stop, twenty-four hours a day — and not just anyone off the street could get involved. This was serious stuff. One has to register before the bidding starts, and if the person has played the game before they must use their earlier login and password to place bids. They would log on to www.scpauctions.com and click on the Registration tab, enter all the required information, and then click on Register at the bottom of the page. During this registration process, they would create their own login — an email address — and password.

Then they would receive an email confirming the registration, and that is when they would be asked to provide two industry trade references. If they didn't have an established account with SCP Auctions, rest assured that the company would contact those references to approve the account and the person's bidding status. This was effectively a screening process to ensure that only serious buyers would be playing such a big-stakes game.

All the bidding was done on the Internet. For this auction, things began on April 30th, 2012 at 10 a.m. PST (1 p.m. EST), with bidding scheduled to close on Saturday, May 19th at 7 p.m. PST (10 p.m. EST). Pacific Standard Times were listed first because SCP Auctions is based on the west coast in California. Those doing the bidding would hail from all over the United States, and there would also be international bidders from other countries. Who exactly were these people? The folks who run SCP Auctions, Lelands and other companies involved never reveal such information. It remains classified. But they do say that the auctions attract everyone from ordinary folk who are serious collectors to very wealthy individuals. That means professionals, especially lawyers, not to mention celebrities, movie stars, what have you.

When an item is up for sale — everything is done online — the entire auction remains open and stays open until fifteen minutes pass without a bid being placed. When that happens, the auction closes down, but according to the schedule this wouldn't take place until the evening of May 19th. For each and every item, bids would increase by increments of 10% and the highest bidder would be awarded the goods. Then it's just a matter of processing the payment and the shipping.

All auctions come with a catalogue and this one was no different.

The 244-page catalogue for the May, 2012 Premier Internet Auction contained every item that was up for sale. The cover of the catalogue displayed an old New York Yankee jersey — *that one*, the circa 1920 jersey — as well as a ball signed by Babe Ruth, two Louisville Slugger bats with the name of guess who carved into the wood, a postcard with his autograph, an inscribed photo that said '*Good luck from Babe Ruth 5-17-48*', and a photograph of an older Ruth in his Yankees uniform.

On the surface it would appear that this was pretty much going to be a Babe Ruth affair, and while the Babe was certainly king of the show — virtually everyone in the business says that is the case — the auction had items from other athletes as well. The May, 2012 Premier Internet Auction included such collectibles as a 1954 Henry Aaron rookie card that would eventually sell for $357,594 and a 1955 Roberto Clemente rookie card that would fetch $432,690. In addition, the auction posted a 1968 New York Yankee road jersey autographed by Mickey Mantle ($366,967), a home jersey circa 1931 that was worn by Lou Gehrig ($275,706), the baseball cap worn by Bobby Thomson when he slugged his Shot Heard 'Round the World home run that won the 1951 National League pennant ($173,102), and a Jackie Robinson All-Star bat from 1950 ($133,234).

Sports memorabilia Internet auctions are not for the faint of heart, nor are they for those not well-heeled.

And so, the New York Yankee jersey from the early '20s wasn't the only Ruth item listed. Another much-desired article of clothing was a cap that he had worn a decade later. It was from the 1930-1933 period and would wind up selling for $537,278, making it the highest price ever fetched for a baseball cap. Former Yankees pitcher David Wells, an ardent admirer of Ruth with a sizeable tattoo of the Bambino at bat on his forearm, once bought that same cap for a measly $35,000. That was back in 1997. Wells actually wore the cap at Yankee Stadium in a league game against the Cleveland Indians on June 28th in the 1997 season, much to the chagrin of Yankee manager Joe Torre who would later fine the pitcher $2,500 for his antics.

Wells didn't much care. During the fifteen years that he owned the Ruth cap, it had appreciated in value by about 1,500%, which works out to 100% a year. The fact that Wells actually wore it in a real game at the same stadium where Ruth once played was worthwhile back-story that only added to its value.

Yet another Ruth artifact in the auction was a bat that he had used in the 1920s. It would sell for $591,007. More than a million bucks for a bat and a cap? That's right. It is Babe Ruth, remember? Still, these items would turn out to be chicken feed compared to the jersey.

At the time, the world record for any item of sports memorabilia was $4,338,500, which was for the original rules of basketball written by the game's inventor, Dr. James Naismith. That sale had been con-summated two years earlier in 2010.

The historic document had been written in 1891. Naismith, a Canadian who was teaching at the YMCA in Springfield, Massachusetts at the time, wrote up thirteen rules of the new game of basketball on two separate pages, and signed his name to each page. The original rules had been owned by Ian Naismith, grandson of the game's inven-tor, and the buyers were a Kansas couple who had the money. Ian Naismith died in March, 2012, while his grandfather had passed away in 1939. After expenses, the proceeds from the sale wound up going to the Naismith International Basketball Foundation, a non-profit organization that helped disadvantaged children.

Like all items in the May, 2012 Premier Internet Auction, the Babe Ruth jersey came on board with a minimum bid. A starting point. That minimum or starting bid was set at $250,000 and it didn't take long for the price to rise. As the rules specify, bids would rise at incre-ments of 10%, and on the first day of the auction a second bid came in at $275,000 and pretty soon they were at $500,000.

Half a million.

Several days later bidding hit the $1-million mark, and according to the rules of the auction, when that happens for an item further bids would thereafter increase by margins of 5%. It wasn't long before the

The world-record jersey with other Babe Ruth items which sold at auction.
They include a 1927 baseball signed by Ruth and Lou Gehrig ($34,243),
1927-1928 game-used bat ($591,007), 1932 game-used bat ($56,500),
rare 8x10 autographed photo ($5,026), autographed Yankee Stadium
postcard signed on Babe Ruth Day on April 27, 1947 ($11,306), circa 1928
Babe Ruth's own book of baseball store advertising display ($2,082),
and photo from Culver Pictures archives ($519).]

bidding for the jersey was up to $2 million. The days marched on, the auction wound down, and the pace of bidding for the jersey kept heating up. Over the last day and night it would turn into a virtual frenzy.

As with any SCP auction, things wouldn't stop until fifteen minutes pass with no bids on any items, and this time around that wouldn't happen until the wee hours of Sunday morning, May 20th. The May, 2012 Premier Internet Auction was going beyond the scheduled closing time, which was supposed to happen on the Saturday evening. But then this wasn't just any auction.

The executives at SCP Auctions and Lelands all stayed up late. Mike Heffner of Lelands, who had that Mystery Buyer on his mind all the time, was bidding by computer on the jersey from his hotel room in Cleveland, Ohio. He had been attending a sports memorabilia show. Did he get nervous as the price kept rising? Not really. The only thing that frayed on his mind was the possibility of losing out on the jersey that he so much wanted to buy. It wasn't the money.

Heffner would later confide that, when the auction began, he figured the jersey might go as high as $3 million and he was prepared to bid that much. He knew of collectors who would be interested in buying the jersey from Lelands, and of course, one of them in particular — the Mystery Buyer — was especially keen. And so, the bidding kept going up in the early hours that Sunday morning. Heffner had set his alarm clock to ensure that he would be in on the action when push came to shove, and through those early hours of Sunday morning he would stay glued to his computer screen. In fact, he placed several bids on the jersey. It was around 4 a.m. that Sunday morning when he would place the 36th and final bid that would ultimately win him the item. That bid was for $4,415,658, which included the standard buyer's premium of 20%. The fifteen minutes then passed and the auction was over. Lelands was now official owner of the jersey.

"It was very competitive," Heffner said later as he rationalized why anyone would spend so much money on a baseball jersey. "You actually lose sight of the value of something when you're in this business. You just don't want to lose the thing. There are people who pay hundreds of millions of dollars for a painting. Well, Babe Ruth was an artist. He hit home runs. Was I shocked that the jersey went for that much money? No. Surprised, but not shocked."

Did he ever fear that his company might be in danger of going under? After all, we are talking almost $4.5 million here. No. Not for a moment. Heffner was a player who knew the market inside out. He personally had authenticated tens of millions of dollars' worth of sports memorabilia over the years, and had even consulted for the FBI on fakes and frauds, which today remains an ongoing problem in the industry. He had started at Lelands when he was still in college and had worked his way up to President. He possessed a trained eye for quality and condition, and was a man who knew a thing or two about value.

Heffner knew there were a few dozen people out there willing to pay millions of dollars for this Babe Ruth jersey, and after his company had the item in its possession, he did receive a number of calls. He even had offers of *more* than the $4.4 million that his company had paid, but Lelands already had an agreement in place with the Mystery Buyer; the agreement was that this person had first right of refusal and that's where the jersey went.

The prize Ruth jersey was promptly sold to the Mystery Buyer.

"It's a niche market," said Heffner at the time. "And five years from now that jersey will be worth $10 million."

Five years later in 2017 Heffner was asked how much that jersey would go for — it was still no. 1, the Guinness World Record holder — and this is what he said: "There's no way telling what it's worth until you auction it but my educated guess is that it's worth upwards of $10 million now."

When the 2012 auction was over and the sale was done, Lelands made sure to pre-pay for the jersey before taking delivery — that was standard procedure — and then the jersey was taken out of its vault at the SCP Auctions building in Laguna Niguel, California, and shipped across the country. And certainly not by FedEx. When it comes to transporting such valuable commodities, SCP Auctions turns to trained and armed guards. Think of a company like Brinks transporting gold bullion from one location to another. As it turned out, the vintage jersey would be personally delivered by a former Secret Service agent who owned a company that dealt with things like this.

"You be careful with that," SCP's David Kohler told the man when he took possession of the jersey.

"I protected presidents," was the response.

"Presidents can be replaced," said Kohler. "This jersey can't."

With the momentous sale, a new world record had just been set for an item of sports memorabilia. The jersey had outsold Naismith's original rules of basketball by $77,158. One week after the auction was over, Kohler got a call from the people at Guinness World Records for all the juicy details, and yes, he did do a lot of interviews with the media.

In total, SCP's May, 2012 Premier Internet Auction sold more than $12 million worth of sports memorabilia — a record — and more than one-third of that sum was for a single item. The Babe Ruth jersey. The jersey was special. It sold for almost *twice* what it cost to build Yankee Stadium in 1923. The original tab for that stadium had been $2.4 million. But when you're talking Babe Ruth, everything is removed from the norm. It is just a whole new ball game and it begs the question.

Why is Babe Ruth so valuable and why does anything associated with the man keep increasing in value?

Says Leland's Heffner: "Babe Ruth reminds us of the way it used to be when baseball players were not enhancing their skills with drugs so people today can gain more of an understanding of baseball with his natural abilities. He really saved the game and his legend grows every year. His legacy will continue to grow."

Heffner went on. He says the industry of sports memorabilia and cards has been growing steadily every year for the past thirty years, and that it now is a billion-dollar business. That's right. *Billion*. And he says Babe Ruth stands at the top of the heap.

But there is more to the why.

Says Heffner: "He was a nice, compassionate human being and we don't see that much anymore. The fact is if Babe Ruth touches something it turns to gold. A bat. A ball. Anything that's related to him."

*"He laid the foundation for the game of baseball
to become a significant part of Japan's national culture."*
— *Ryozo Kato, former Japanese ambassador to the U.S.
and former Commissioner of Nippon Professional Baseball*

Chapter 10

THE BABE RUTH EFFECT

IN 1931 A TEAM of professional baseball players from the United States visited Japan and it wasn't the first time. While the trip would be deemed a success, Babe Ruth wasn't part of it. In fact, attempts had been made as early as 1929 to get him to come to the country, but in 1934 it finally happened and that changed everything. Baseball in Japan would never be the same again.

The trip with American League all-stars was sponsored by the *Yomiuri Shimbun* newspaper and came to fruition after the end of the 1934 season. Without question, the key was Ruth. The 1934 season turned out to be his last with the Yankees — that year the thirty-nine-year-old Ruth hit only twenty-two home runs and had a .288 batting average — but on the trip to Japan he looked to be anything but washed up. Not only was he the field manager of the team, but during the eighteen-game series he would lead his squad in every hitting category — .408 batting average, thirty-three runs batted in, twenty-seven runs scored, and what was most impressive of all, especially to the Japanese, thirteen home runs. When it was over he had more than left his mark in the country and had established himself as the chief American ambassador.

After the tour the U.S. ambassador to Japan said as much. Ambassador Joseph C. Grew wrote in his diary of November 6, 1934: "All Japan has gone wild over him. He is a great deal more effective ambassador than I could ever be."[40]

After the tour in Japan, the American team went on to Shanghai, China to play against a team of Chinese, and followed that up with three more games in Manila in the Philippines. In the Philippines Ruth hit another home run.

By the time 1934 rolled around Japanese newspapers had already been covering the World Series for more than ten years and several American professional teams had visited the country, but 1934 was the big one. Until that time the very concept of professional baseball carried a negative connotation in Japan; baseball just wasn't something you were paid to do. Not according to the Japanese.

Along with Ruth the all-stars included such names as his Yankee teammates Lou Gehrig and Lefty Gomez, Jimmy Foxx of the Athletics and several members of that club, and other prominent players. They would play a series of exhibition games against Japanese all-stars and the Americans wound up winning all eighteen games. Ruth himself describes the trip in the book *The Babe Ruth Story* by Babe Ruth and Bob Considine (E. P. Dutton & Company, 1948):

'We played mostly college teams and a team of Japanese All-Stars.
I was surprised at their high-class fielding and the ability of some
of their pitchers. But they couldn't hit a lick. We won most of our
games by top-heavy scores, but that didn't discourage the crowds.
They filled every stadium, and the fields at Tokyo and Kobe are
bigger than anything we have outside of the Yankee Stadium and the
one at Cleveland.'[41]

Nevertheless, the fans went crazy, and they went especially crazy for Ruth.

Indeed, the arrival in port of the ocean liner the Empress of Japan, which carried the American team, resulted in a huge traffic jam with thousands upon thousands of bicycles and rickshaws. When the Americans hit Tokyo there was a motorcade parade in the Ginza district of the city with all the American players in cars. Estimates claim that 500,000 people lined up to greet them and maybe more than that. Julia, eighteen at the time, was also there with her mother Claire and says he was greeted *like a God*.

Baseball historian Robert K. Fitts, a leading authority on baseball in Japan who lived for a time in Tokyo, says as much in his book

Banzai Babe Ruth (University of Nebraska Press, Lincoln and London, 2012). The book is all about the 1934 tour and describes in detail the kind of reception Ruth got.

'The streets of the financial district had been lined with fans, waving flags and shouting 'Banzai,'' but they were just an opening act for the crowd in Ginza. Here hundreds of thousands packed the sidewalks, spilling onto the streets, blocking traffic and trolleys. With nowhere to go, passengers disembarked, joining the throng. The crowd included businessmen, old and young, dressed in suits and fedoras; students in the military-style black uniforms and peaked hats covering their nearly shaved heads; workmen in their jackets and baggy *tobi* trousers with their thick bifurcated socks called *jika-tabi* that they wore instead of boots; soldiers in their khaki uniforms and narrow caps; street urchins in mismatching shirts and pants; young women in kimonos with their hair pulled back into tight buns; and women in Western dresses, their hair cut in a bob. They were all there, jostling, pushing, shouting, trying to get a better view of Ruth — the God of Baseball.

"Banzai! Banzai, Babe Ruth!" they screamed.'[42]

Banzai, which literally means 'ten thousand years of life to you,' is more akin to such a phrase as 'long live the king' and there was no doubt who was king on this trip. In his book Fitts related what the American press thought about it all.

"Tokyo Gives Ruth Royal Welcome" blared the *New York Times* on November 3. The Associated Press article, picked up by newspapers across the globe, continued, "The Babe's big bulk today blotted out such unimportant things as international squabbles over oil and navies." Many observers considered the all-stars' joyous reception proof that the two countries' differences could be reconciled. *The Chicago Daily Tribune* neatly summed up this argument in its lead sentence: "Diplomats and admirals are arguing over oil and navies, but the Japanese populace found a common ground of agreement today with Americans — baseball and Babe Ruth."[43]

Exactly how many people showed up that day remains open to debate, but those who have written about it say *one million* is not out of the question.

Japanese businessman and publisher Matsutaro Shoriki received much of the credit for organizing the 1934 tour. The aforementioned sportswriter Bob Considine, who was a prominent Ruth aficionado, wrote about Shoriki in the Foreword to the book *Matsutaro Shoriki — Miracle Man of Japan* by Edward Uhlan and Dana L. Thomas (Exposition Press, New York, 1957). Said Considine of Shoriki:

> 'In the publishing field he was called "the William Randolph Hearst of Japan" for decades. In baseball he was, at first, "the Judge Landis and Colonel Jake Ruppert of Japanese baseball" and in later years "the Ford Frick" and whichever American club-owner was current and choice.'[44]

One chapter in *Matsutaro Shoriki — Miracle Man of Japan is called Babe Ruth Comes to Japan* and went into detail about the impact Ruth had in Tokyo:

> 'The Babe Ruth team arrived at Yokohama on the Empress of Japan on November 2, 1934. The dock was jammed with eager Japanese baseball fans. In Tokyo the team was paraded down the Ginza in open cars, Ruth riding in the first. That was a mistake. The fans crowded so thickly around his automobile that the whole caval- cade was halted. The newspapers said more than a million people crowded onto the Ginza that day to see Babe Ruth.
>
> 'Ruth reacted magnificently and won the hearts of the Japanese. He had played to tremendous crowds in America, but never did he play before as many as the 100,000 who pushed and shoved their way into Meijii Stadium in Tokyo. Ruth did everything right.
>
> 'One full nine-inning game was played in a drenching rain. But Ruth said that as long as the fans would sit in the stands in the downpour to see him, the least he could do was play it out.

The American League All-Stars on their tour of Japan in 1934

'Ruth played first base that day and Gehrig was in left field. During the first inning, a fan climbed out of the stands and handed Ruth his umbrella. The game was halted briefly while Ruth and the fan exchanged courteous bows, Ruth clowning it a bit. Through the rest of the game, Ruth stood at first base holding his umbrella.

'The rest of the players took their cue from Ruth and went up into the stands to ask other Japanese to lend them umbrellas. They got them. And one fan even gave Gehrig a pair of rubber boots. Gehrig took off his spikes and played the rest of the game in boots.

'The only ones who did not get into the act were the pitcher, Earl Whitehill, and the catcher, Moe Berg. It just wasn't feasible to hold an umbrella while pitching or catching.

'After the [final game] Ruth called the full team out to home plate and made a brief speech of thanks to the Japanese fans. The

Japanese never forgot Ruth. In 1947, after World War II, they designated April 27 as Babe Ruth Day in professional baseball. And a Babe Ruth plaque adorns the main entrance of Koshien Stadium in Osaka, Japan's biggest baseball park.'[45]

During the tour the stadiums couldn't hold all the people who wanted to get in to watch. Once, when the Americans were having a practice, more than 20,000 people showed up to see them. For a practice! Indeed, a game in the city of Shizuoka attracted some 200,000 people who tried to get in, but the stadium had only 20,000 seats.

Today Koshien Stadium in Osaka is the oldest and most historical baseball stadium in Japan. It is home to the Hanshin Tigers who play in the Central League of Nippon Professional Baseball which is the highest level of professional baseball in the country. The stadium was built way back in 1924. The bronze plaque with the likeness of Ruth reads:

In Memory of BABE RUTH. 1895-1948. Who played at Koshien Stadium in 1934.

As impressive as that might be, an even more profound memory of Ruth's visit to Japan is relatively recent. In 2002 a statue of Ruth went up in Yagiyama Zoological Park in Sendai City. The statue was erected on the very spot where Ruth hit his first home run on that 1934 tour. It had happened at Miyagi Prefecture Yagiyama Baseball Stadium on November 4, 1934. In fact, he swatted two home runs that day. The ground is now part of the zoological park. What's more, funding for the statue and the commemorative plaque accompanying it came from donations from local citizens. A committee called 'Let's Build a Babe Ruth Statue in Former Yagiyama Field' was dedicated to getting it done. The inscription on that one reads:

This bronze statue stands as a witness, to future generations, of Sendai's part in Japanese-American baseball history.

The 1934 tour of the American League all-stars is widely regarded as the impetus for professional baseball in Japan, and Ruth was the main reason. Ryozo Kato, former Japanese ambassador to the United States and a man who also served as head of Japanese professional baseball, says so himself. In fact, he calls this "the Babe Ruth effect." Kato was Japan's ambassador to the U.S. from 2001 to 2008, and when he left public life he became Commissioner of Nippon Professional Baseball. He held that post until 2013.

A lifelong baseball fan, Kato says baseball has served as a bridge between Japan and the United States ever since it was first introduced to the country in 1872 by Horace Wilson, an English teacher who taught at a Japanese school in Tokyo. But Kato credits Ruth with opening the door and paving the way.

"In retrospect he prompted and led Japan to create professional baseball which is the number one sport in Japan today," says Kato. "The 1934 visit of Major League Baseball to Japan with ultra-superstar Babe Ruth on the team opened up a new page in Japan's baseball history. Babe Ruth was, as he himself noted, treated like a King. His visit had a cultural impact on the minds of Japanese. The most important thing about Babe Ruth in terms of his impact on Japan is the fact that he laid the foundation for the game of baseball to become a significant part of Japan's national culture."

Kato says that over the past eighty years Ruth has been 'the legend' for Japanese baseball fans. "His name is monumental," he says.

There is a photograph from June 5, 1948 of an ailing Ruth donating the manuscript of his book *The Babe Ruth Story* to the Yale Library at Yale University. In the photo he is shown presenting the manuscript to the captain of Yale's college baseball team. That captain, who played first base, was none other than George H. W. Bush, who forty years later would become the 41st President of the United States. Kato says he knows the photo well and he should — he himself is an alumnus of Yale — and is quick to point out that both the senior Bush, and George W. Bush, the 43rd President of the United States, are both

A young George H. W. Bush and Babe Ruth

big baseball fans. The younger Bush was once an owner of the Texas Rangers baseball club.

Kato has lots of stories about meeting baseball luminaries over the years. The list includes such stars as Joe DiMaggio, but he has a special memory from the days when he was Japan's Ambassador to the United States. It happened in St. Louis. Says Kato: "I had lunch with Stan Musial and I remember him telling me about the time when he met Babe Ruth. I can tell you that Babe Ruth was a great hero to Stan Musial."

After the 1934 tour there was a lot of interest in getting professional baseball off the ground in Japan. While there had been a couple pro teams in the 1920s, they didn't survive, but the arrival of Ruth and the Americans had tremendous impact. Author Robert K. Fitts says Ruth became a symbol to the Japanese of what was good about America, and pro baseball was also good for business. Circulation of the *Yomiuri Shimbun* newspaper, which was the sponsor, hit new heights during the tour with the stadiums packed for every game. The Japanese team was kept together and the next year it traveled to the United States to play against American teams, including professional minor-league squads.

Robert Whiting is a best-selling author and journalist who has written many books about Japan, a number of them on baseball. A resident of California who also maintains a home in Tokyo, he acknowledges that while American pro teams had come to Japan before 1934, none of them had Babe Ruth in the lineup.

"Because he was there in 1934 it made the idea of professional baseball more popular," says Whiting. "Everyone had a lot of fun on that trip. It was a big love-fest. Ruth played to the fans and the press just like he always did in America."

A well-known photograph of Ruth has him in that memorable game in the pouring rain when the Japanese fans felt bad for him and someone handed him an umbrella. So there he was, an aged (for a ballplayer) and paunchy Babe Ruth, slightly stooped over and waiting for the next pitch, his right hand in a glove, his left hand holding up this umbrella resting on his shoulder.

The fans loved it.

The Japanese press couldn't get enough of him. Japanese sports-writer Sotaro Suzuki is the one who had persuaded an initially reluctant Ruth to come to the country after showing him a poster with his face on it. In the poster Ruth actually appears to be Asian. In 1935, a few months after the tour, Suzuki told the *Sporting News* about the impact Ruth had on Japan. He said: "Practically every kid in Japan now wants to emulate Babe Ruth."[46]

The onset of World War II could have soured Ruth's name in Japan, but that didn't happen. At one time the battle cry of Japanese soldiers charging American troops was "To hell with Babe Ruth" because nothing could have been deemed more insulting to the Americans. It wasn't the name of Abraham Lincoln or George Washington they wanted to sully. It was Babe Ruth. But, if anything, this was a sign of respect, and in the waning days of the war in the Pacific the U.S. State Department even considered sending radio messages from none other than Babe Ruth to the people of Japan, asking them to lay down their arms.

Ruth himself was furious over the attack at Pearl Harbor on December 7, 1941, but after the war he spoke with great affection about the Japanese, and did so in true Babe Ruth fashion:

> 'Despite the treacherous attack the Japs made on us only seven years later, I cannot help but feel that the reception which millions of Japs gave us was genuine. They lined the streets of the Ginza, the Broadway of Tokyo, for miles and greeted us as though we were real heroes. Everywhere we went they feted us and tried to make our stay pleasant. No doubt there were plenty of stinkers among them, but looking back at that visit I feel it is another example of how a crackpot government can lead a friendly people into war.'[47]

The 1934 tour was a long time ago, but the *Babe Ruth effect* lingers to this day. On April 9, 2017, the CBS flagship news show *60 Minutes* did a feature on Japan's rising baseball star Shohei Ohtani who, according to the reporter, could be the first Major League Baseball player in a hundred years to figure in a team's starting rotation *and* its everyday lineup. The last one to do that was Ruth. Alas, the young Ohtani is both a pitcher and a hitter. The feature was called 'Is Japan's Babe Ruth headed to the majors?'

In the *60 Minutes* interview, Ohtani was asked how he felt about being compared to Babe Ruth. Through an interpreter he said:

> "He's like a mythical character to me because it's such a long time ago and he was God to baseball."

Babe Ruth may have been God to baseball, but for the Japanese his influence went far beyond the sport. Kazuo Sayama, a leading

This photo of Ryozo Kato, center, was taken in 2012
when he was Commissioner of Nippon Professional Baseball.
On his right is Tomoyuki Sugano, who was pitcher of the year in 2017,
and on his left is Shohei Ohtani whose nickname is 'Japan's Babe Ruth'
because of his talent as a pitcher and a power hitter. Ohtani joined
Major League Baseball for the 2018 season.

baseball historian in Japan, attended the 1995 Babe Ruth conference
at Hofstra University and presented a paper called 'The Impact of
Babe Ruth on Japan and Japanese Culture.' It was one of many papers
delivered at that conference, but the organizers were impressed; that
year Sayama received the school's Dr. Joseph G. Astman Award for
his paper. The annual award is named after the man who established
the Hofstra Cultural Center as a forum for 'international scholarly
thought.' In his award-winning paper Sayama said the impact of Babe
Ruth could be explained on three fronts:

1. He accelerated the formation of a Japanese professional
    baseball league.

2. He made a drastic change in the Japanese notion of sports in general.

3. He helped slacken the tension then present between the United States and Japan.

Sayama said that before organized baseball there were no real team sports in Japan and that 'Babe Ruth caused a great change in the Japanese notion toward sports in general.' This is how he explained the Ruth phenomenon in his paper:

'It was the Babe's visit that changed this notion of the Japanese toward sports. He showed by his performances that baseball could be — and should be — an enjoyment. He showed by his behavior that he himself was enjoying baseball, and that he wanted spectators to share the enjoyment. Even his funny deeds on the diamond, which had been regarded as a sacred place, were looked upon as the expression of his amiable personality. He had already shown his love for Japan and the Japanese people. He couldn't have intended to do anything insulting to the Japanese.

'When he landed at Yokohama pier, the first thing Babe did was to go to a group of blind children who were lined up there in baseball uniforms to welcome the party. The schoolmaster, Ikuta Inamura, had devised a special baseball for the blind, and the blind children were the players. Babe not only took them up in his arms, but also encouraged other American players to do the same. His personality was evident upon his arrival, and the Japanese loved everything he did.

'His joyful way of playing baseball had a greater influence than anything else in changing the Japanese way of engaging in sports. He showed the Japanese a very simple way of enjoying games, quite far from the old, stoic attitude.

'Babe Ruth's influence on the Japanese was not limited to the baseball field alone. He contributed much to the Japanese understanding of the American people. Various publications told about his personality and background. His life story as a fulfillment of the American dream attracted many Japanese. And, in reality, his every deed in Japan was true to the legend. Many Japanese had the chance to know about America through him and had respect for the society in which he lived.'

There was one other thing that Sayama said about Ruth's impact in the country, and it had to do with money and the reading habits of the Japanese. A prime objective of that 1934 trip was for newspaper publisher Matsutaro Shoriki to increase the circulation of his newspaper, and with Babe Ruth, he did. Again, in his Hofstra paper which was presented in 1995, Sayama explained:

'Babe Ruth could be said to have encouraged the Japanese public to read newspapers, which until then was the domain of the intellectuals. Today the *Yomiuri* enjoys the greatest circulation of any newspaper in the whole world. The latest edition of *The Guinness Book of Records* rates the *Yomiuri* as the number one newspaper, with a circulation of 10,074,678 for the morning paper and 4,482,852 for the evening paper. All told, the current circulation is 14,557,537 (as of July 1994). That means one out of every 4.3 Japanese families reads the newspaper daily. At the beginning of this great success was Babe Ruth, the Sultan of Swat.'

Ruth's celebrated Banzai portrait still hangs in the Japanese Baseball Hall of Fame and Museum in Tokyo. In terms of books, there is no shortage of works that have been translated into Japanese or written only in Japanese on the subject of all things Ruthian.

Notwithstanding the impact that Ruth had on Japan, the *Babe Ruth effect* goes far beyond the shores of that country. Today more than one-quarter of all the players who play in Major League Baseball were born outside the United States and that proportion is increasing. Of those non-U.S. countries, the only ones currently with more than one hundred major-league players are from the Dominican Republic and Venezuela. But next on the list is Cuba.

At the 1995 Hofstra University conference on Babe Ruth a history professor from Plymouth State University, University System of New Hampshire, presented a paper called *Babe Ruth's Impact on Latin American Baseball and Latin American Ballplayers: Cuba — A Case Study*. The paper, by Manuel Marquez-Sterling, began like this:

'In many foreign countries, at some point in time, many American products became synonymous with the United States of America, to name a few, RCA radio and victrolas, the Model 'T' Ford, Packard, Cadillac, and Parker pens. Babe Ruth and Baseball can be added to this list, especially for those Latin American countries in which the game of "Beisbol" is played. In fact, for legions of Latin American fans and Latin American players, Babe Ruth was the United States and the United States, Babe Ruth.'

Marquez-Sterling hails from a prominent political family. His father Carlos ran for President of Cuba in 1958 and went into exile after Fidel Castro took over. The younger Marquez-Sterling was born and raised in Cuba, and moved with his family to the United States in 1960. He became a history professor, and while he has written much about politics, he has also long maintained an avid interest in baseball.

His paper at Hofstra discussed Ruth's barnstorming trip to Cuba in 1920 and mentioned how, at first, there was a reluctance to embrace the home run in Cuban baseball, preferring the small ball of Ty Cobb, who had also barnstormed in the country. It wasn't until American player Dick Sisler, son of Hall of Famer George Sisler, went to play for the Havana Lions in 1946 and immediately started smashing home runs that the home run became widely accepted. Wrote Marquez-Sterling:

'We can conclude that Ruthian baseball entered Cuban baseball in a delayed fashion and only when the social, economic and political conditions were apt and propitious in the country.'

For his research into how much influence Ruth had, Marquez-Sterling made a study of Cuban magazines and newspapers from 1908 through 1935, the year Ruth retired. He also mailed a questionnaire to fifty baseball players and they included not only Cubans but also Puerto Ricans, Dominicans, Venezuelans and Mexicans. Replies were not as numerous as he had hoped, but of those who did respond, he made this observation:

> 'These responses, with the exception of a couple, seem to have been under the spell of Ruth's image and legend as it projected on the Cuba of the last '30s and early '40s. This is succinctly and aptly stated by one of the respondents. "All of us, in our times, tried in one way or another to imitate him, especially hitting home runs."'

But Ruth's impact on Cuba may have involved more than home runs. In 1918 the Cuban Stars from Havana, an all-black team, was touring the United States and playing against semi-pro and Minor League teams. Those teams were all white. The Cubans were good, so good that they won thirty of thirty-two games against their opponents. George Weiss, who owned the New Haven Colonials in the Eastern League, a minor-pro circuit, got the Cubans to come to his park but realized his team might be in over its head. And he was right. They were. So he called Babe Ruth whose season was done because his Boston Red Sox had just won the World Series. The two men knew each other; earlier that season Weiss had persuaded Ruth and the Red Sox to come to New Haven for an exhibition game.

Segregation was a big deal in the highest levels of American professional baseball at the time, but that didn't deter from Ruth joining Weiss's New Haven Colonials for the game. He wanted to play against the Cubans. Baseball historian Bill Jenkinson has written about the significance of that event, and says it had more to do with race than home runs. He wrote an essay called *Babe Ruth and the Issue of Race* and this is what he said:

> 'When Weiss extended the invitation for Ruth to return to New Haven to play the "ebony skinned" Cubans, Babe "jumped at the opportunity." Predictably, the Stars whipped the Colonials handily,

but Ruth provided the only bright light in the 5-1 defeat with a mammoth homer beyond the flagpole in left centerfield. I believe, however, that the day's events transcended sports.

'At that moment, Babe Ruth was in the process of supplanting Ty Cobb (a man of questionable racial sensitivity) as the pre-eminent baseball player in America. When he unhesitatingly agreed to take the field against performers of African descent, he sent a powerful signal that could not be ignored. As was usually the case in whatever he did, Ruth kept moving forward in the matter of race relations. After being sold to the New York Yankees in 1920, Babe took the final step in becoming baseball's unquestioned kingpin by walloping fifty-four homers. That was an astounding accomplishment for that era.

'When the season ended, Ruth received hundreds of invitations to barnstorm anywhere he wanted to go. Of the approximately fifteen games that Babe selected, five were against so-called Negro League teams. Ruth then sailed to Cuba, where he joined John McGraw's Giants to play nine more contests versus a combination of Latino and Negro ballplayers. Again, the message was clear: if the sports' transcendent figure played without reservation against Black ballplayers, why shouldn't everyone else?'

'However, at the same time, another powerful but opposing dynamic was taking shape. As a result of the "Black Sox Scandal" of 1919, Judge Kenesaw Landis was being wooed by MLB owners to take over as commissioner. He assumed office on January 12, 1921, and was provided with nearly dictatorial power. Landis was a complex man of contrasting traits, but even his staunchest admirers find it difficult to defend his record on race relations. Essentially, he did nothing for twenty-four years (he died on November 25, 1944) to advance the cause of integration in Major League Baseball. Accordingly, while Babe Ruth was knocking down the color barriers in autumn 1920, Landis was seemingly content to maintain them.'

The color barrier in Major League Baseball wasn't broken until 1947 when Jackie Robinson joined the Brooklyn Dodgers, but as far as professional baseball in North America is concerned, it had happened one year prior to that. In Canada. That same Robinson played the full 1946 season with the AAA Montreal Royals, a farm team of the Dodgers, and led the league in hitting with a .346 batting average. The next year with the Dodgers he was Rookie of the Year and in his third season he was the National League's Most Valuable Player. Baseball executive Branch Rickey is credited for bringing Robinson up to the big leagues.

Breaking the color barrier for professional baseball was a major development and Canada played its part, but Canada also has a number of intriguing connections to Babe Ruth, and some of them are not well known.

The man who first taught Ruth how to play baseball, Brother Matthias at St. Mary's Industrial School in Baltimore, was a Canadian who hailed from Cape Breton Island in Nova Scotia. His real name was Martin Boutlier. Brother Matthias was the superintendent, the man in charge of discipline at St. Mary's. Ruth first attended the institution at the age of seven and wound up spending all his formative years there until he was nineteen when he became a professional baseball player. What kind of impact did this man have on the young Ruth? In his celebrated biography on Babe Ruth, author Robert W. Creamer wrote:

'Ruth revered Brother Matthias — "He was the greatest man I've ever known," he would often say.'[48]

It has been mentioned in some circles that Ruth's first wife, Helen Woodford, was also a Nova Scotia native, but there is debate on that point. Suffice to say that her family may have had Nova Scotia roots. However, a definite Canadian connection did exist in the historic transaction that took Ruth from the Boston Red Sox to the New York Yankees. The Royal Bank of Canada was involved in the deal which included a $125,000 cheque and a $300,000 bond. The bond was financed through the bank's agency in New York.

Of more significance is the city of Toronto laying claim to Ruth's first home run. In this case, it was his first professional home run in an official league game. That occurred on September 5, 1914, when Ruth was a rookie pitcher with the AAA Providence Grays and not long removed from his days at St. Mary's. On that day, a mere three weeks after the outbreak of World War I, Ruth was pitching against the Toronto Maple Leafs baseball team and clubbed a home run. It would be his one and only home run in the minor leagues.

It happened at an old ballpark at Hanlan's Point on the Toronto Islands, off the city's mainland. Today the Toronto chapter of SABR (Society of American Baseball Research) is aptly named the Hanlan's Point chapter. In 2006 the site of that home run, now an airport, was the focus for a commemorative plaque in a ceremony involving representatives of the Toronto Blue Jays and New York Yankees. The inscription at the top of the plaque says *BABE RUTH AT HANLAN'S POINT* and reads as follows:

> *Near this site, in Maple Leaf Park on September 5, 1914, the now legendary baseball player Babe Ruth hit his first home run as a professional. It was to be the only home run he ever hit in the minor leagues.*

> *As a 19-year-old rookie, playing for the Providence Grays in the International League, he connected with a pitch from Ellis Johnson of the Toronto Maple Leafs, sending the ball over the fence in right field and scoring three runs. Pitching for the Grays, Ruth allowed only one hit, earning the title "southside phenom" from the Toronto Daily Star. The final score was Providence Grays 9, Toronto Maple Leafs 0.*

> *Babe Ruth quickly moved up to the major leagues, and played his way to a phenomenal career. The Toronto team went on to win a total of eleven pennants before folding in 1967.*

What exactly happened to that home-run ball is an item of profound interest in the realm of Canadian baseball lore. Some say the ball went over the fence and landed in Lake Ontario. Others say it was caught by a fan in the bleachers. For many years a downtown Toronto bar had a bronzed baseball on display for all its patrons to see with the claim that it was, in fact, that ball from 1914. For what it's worth, Babe Ruth also hit another home run in Toronto long after that first one. It happened in an exhibition game when the Yankees were playing against the AAA Toronto Maple Leafs baseball team, and that ball apparently did go into the lake because Maple Leaf Stadium was right on the water.

Tom Valcke is the former President and CEO of the Canadian Baseball Hall of Fame and Museum, and at one time was director of Canadian scouting for Major League Baseball. He added his voice to the controversy about the 1914 homer with this statement in a newspaper interview:

> "I've heard two stories about the Hanlan's Point home run. The first is that it was hit into the lake. The second is that someone stole the ball and as security chased him away he threw it into the water. But maybe it was the baseball from the '30s that was stolen and tossed in. It would almost make draining the lake worthwhile if two of the Babe's biggest taters are sitting at the bottom."[49]

Canadian baseball historian Bill Humber has written about Ruth's Canadian connections, which include numerous hunting trips to Nova Scotia. As for any legacy he might hold in Canada, Humber offers this: "In the everyday specifics of Ruth's impact on Canadian baseball, the verdict would seem to be limited. In the larger, emotional, charismatic, even mythological perspective, Ruth's role was pre-eminent."

What does he mean by that? Says Humber: "Ruth's presence in Canada was that of a pop culture figure. As such he joined a long list of American entertainers from P.T. Barnum to Elvis and Madonna who have captured the imagination and curiosity of Canadians."

Canada may have been the first country outside the United States that Ruth ever visited, but his international appeal really took off with that 1934 trip to Japan, which as mentioned earlier, also included games in China and the Philippines. One of the players on the trip was Moe Berg, a light-hitting catcher who was anything but all-star caliber. During his fifteen-year career in Major League Baseball — he retired in 1939 — Berg sported a paltry lifetime batting average of .243 and a total of six home runs. In only one season did he ever appear in more than 100 games. But Berg was more than a baseball player. He was a graduate of Princeton University and Columbia Law School. While an educational pedigree like that would make him an anomaly for a ballplayer today, back then he was one of a kind. Berg also spoke at least seven languages, including Japanese, and was added to the roster at the last minute. It was the 1930s and relations between America and Japan were tense.

Alas, Berg was a spy for the U.S. government. Later, in 1943, he would be hired by the Office of Strategic Services and over the next few years and into the 1950s he would perform duties for his country. He was awarded the Medal of Freedom, but turned it down, and only after his death in 1972 did he receive it posthumously. His is the only baseball card on display at the headquarters of the CIA. In 1994 there was a book *The Catcher Was a Spy: The Mysterious Life of Moe Berg* by Nicholas Dawidoff (Vintage Books, New York 1994) and in 2017 a film, *The Catcher Was a Spy*, was made.

But as far as Babe Ruth was concerned, Moe Berg was just a mediocre ballplayer. In Japan he was asked by reporters to comment on Berg's ability to speak so many languages. Ruth remained unfazed. Of Berg he said: "He can speak seven languages, but he can't hit in any of them."[50]

"It wasn't the baseball records that he left us.
It was his legacy of hope."
— author Bill Jenkinson

Chapter 11

THE LEGEND,

THE HERO, THE MAN

Statue of Babe Ruth at
Camden Yards in Baltimore

' I WAS A BAD KID. I say that without pride but with a feeling that it is
   better to say it. Because I live with one great hope in mind: to help
kids who now stand where I stood as a boy. If what I have to say here
helps even one of them avoid some of my own mistakes, or take heart
from such triumphs as I have had, this book will serve its purpose.'[51]

That was the beginning of *The Babe Ruth Story* by Babe Ruth as
told to Bob Considine. In the book Ruth tells how his mother died
when he was thirteen and his father died when he was in his second
year in the majors. He also says, on the next page: 'I hardly knew my
parents.' They had placed him in St. Mary's Industrial School when
he was seven. What were his first seven years like?

'I spent most of the first seven years of my life living over my
father's saloon at 426 West Camden Street in Baltimore. When I
wasn't living over it, I was living in it, studying the rough talk of the
longshoremen, merchant sailors, roustabouts and water-front bums.
When I wasn't living in it, I was living in the neighborhood streets.
I had a rotten start and it took me a long time to get my bearings.'[52]

His youth could have been plucked from a Charles Dickens novel.
Ruth says as a boy he didn't remember being aware of the difference
between right and wrong, but his savior was Brother Matthias at St.
Mary's. Matthias was simply, 'the greatest man I've ever known' and
it wasn't because he taught Ruth how to play baseball. That was secondary. Ruth says he never saw anyone in his life 'who was even close
to Brother Matthias when it came to manliness, kindness and grace.'[53]

Towards the end of the book Ruth talks about 1938 when the
Brooklyn Dodgers coaxed him out of retirement to serve as their first-
base coach:

'One day, beneath the stands at Ebbets Field, I saw a young
Brooklyn player push an autograph-seeking kid roughly out of the

way, and start for the dugout. For what it was worth I said to the boy, "Here, kid, I'll sign it for you," and I said it just loud enough for the player to hear me.'54

And then right after that Ruth adds this observation about life on the road:

'There were a lot of hospitals and orphanages to visit on the trips, too. I always went and I mention it only because I think that the stars of today should take more interest in such things.'55

A foundation was set up in the name of Babe Ruth. In the words of his attorney, Gordon Lowenstein, the purpose was clear: 'The funds will be used to aid American youngsters to achieve good character from participation in sports and to offer scholarships and prizes to underprivileged boys, not necessarily connected with sports.'

What has been said over the years about Babe Ruth?

In 1998 HBO produced the TV documentary *Babe Ruth: The Life Behind the Legend* as part of its Sports of the 20th Century series. The first thing one hears are these words attributed to a former teammate who said: 'If Babe Ruth had not existed it would have been impossible to invent him.'

Said sportswriter Tommy Holmes who covered the Brooklyn Dodgers from 1924 to 1957: "Some twenty years ago I stopped talking about the Babe for the simple reason that I realized that those who had never seen him didn't believe me."56

Broadcaster Ernie Harwell whose career covered fifty-five seasons, most of them with the Detroit Tigers: "He wasn't a baseball player. He was a worldwide celebrity, an international star, the likes of which baseball has never seen since."57

Ruth's Yankee teammate Waite Hoyt: "Every big leaguer and his wife should teach their children to pray, God bless Mommy, God bless Daddy, and God bless Babe Ruth."58

Author, public relations and sports management executive Marty Appel who was born nine days before Ruth died in 1948 and who started working with the New York Yankees twenty years later: "I was able to know a lot of people who knew Babe Ruth and they were universally in awe of his friendship and the man. There was just universal love for the guy. Nobody had a bad word to say about him."

Bill Dickey who played for the Yankees from 1928 to 1943: "He hits the ball harder and farther than any man I ever saw."[59]

One player who may have hit the ball as far was Josh Gibson who was known as 'the black Babe Ruth.' Gibson, regarded far and wide as the best position player in the old Negro leagues, had a youth similar to Ruth's in some ways. Both came from working-class backgrounds and made names for themselves growing up as teenagers playing sandlot ball with amateur teams, Gibson in Pittsburgh and Ruth in Baltimore.

But Gibson was black and Ruth was white.

In 1972 Gibson became the second player from the Negro leagues, after Satchel Paige, to be elected to the National Baseball Hall of Fame. His plaque says that he hit almost 800 home runs in League and Independent baseball during his seventeen-year career. In the 1934 season he hit sixty-nine home runs. Once, when playing for his Homestead Grays against New York's Lincoln Giants in a playoff game at Yankee Stadium, he walloped what some say was the longest home run ever hit at the fabled ball park.

He joined the Homestead Grays at the age of eighteen and less than two weeks after his debut his wife died giving birth to twins. The children were raised by their grandparents while the young Gibson concentrated on his baseball career. He died of a brain tumor in 1947. He was only thirty-five.

How good was he? Walter Johnson, one of the greatest pitchers to ever play the game, said this of Gibson: "There is a catcher that any big league club would like to buy for $200,000. His name is Gibson. He can do everything. He hits the ball a mile. He catches so easy he might as well be in a rocking chair. Throws like a rifle. Too bad this Gibson is a colored fellow."[60]

In 1990 Gibson's son John Gibson Jr. established the Josh Gibson Foundation as an organization to provide scholarships and activities for inner-city youth in Pittsburgh. Today the JGFoundation is run by Sean Gibson, the great-grandson of Josh Gibson. Once, when attending the wedding of a friend, Sean met another invited guest who like him had quite a baseball pedigree — Brent Stevens, son of Tom Stevens, and the great-grandson of Babe Ruth.

"We have stayed in touch," Gibson says. "Brent and I found ways to connect our great-grandfathers. We wanted to educate kids today about them, use them as examples, and focus on civil rights. The idea is to accept people for who they are. Babe Ruth and Josh Gibson never met. They couldn't play together due to racial barriers, but what if they had?"

The two great-grandsons commissioned a painting that depicts Ruth in his Yankee pinstripes standing next to Gibson in his Homestead Grays uniform. It was done by sports artist Bill Purdom. They made high-quality reproductions of the painting in two sizes, a limited run of 300 copies, and put them up for sale. Proceeds went, in part, to the Josh Gibson Foundation and the nonprofit Babe Ruth Scholarship Fund which is administered by Babe Ruth League baseball. It was all done through Legendary Sports Prints, a group of artists who offer original-concept sports art, and the website BabeRuthCentral.com which is a family-run site that pays tribute to the Babe.

Brent Stevens
and Sean Gibson

Brent Stevens started the website with his friend Stu Dressler in 2007 and did it for a reason. He remembers it well. His younger sister was in high school and one day she brought home her American history text book, which had referred to Babe Ruth as a great home run hitter but also an alcoholic and womanizer.

"It infuriated me and motivated me to do something," says Brent. "I

Painting of Babe Ruth and Josh Gibson

learned a lot about the Babe from my grandmother Julia and not only what an amazing baseball player he was, but what a special person he was off the field. The more I got to know the more I realized he is truly one of America's greatest heroes. He is well recognized for his baseball prowess, but what people don't know much about was Babe on a personal level. His constant philanthropy and willingness to give money to people in need that he barely knew. His genuine kindness towards others, particularly children, as well as an appreciation of other races that was way ahead of its time. It all only reinforced the great impression I had of him."

In 1994 Ken Burns released his highly acclaimed television documentary miniseries *Baseball*. The nine-part series included an interview with Buck O'Neil, one of the biggest stars from the Negro Leagues. In the fifth segment, which was called *Inning Five — Shadow Ball*, O'Neil was asked this question: 'Is there one moment in all of baseball you wish you could have seen?'

His response was telling.

"I wish I could have been there when Babe Ruth pointed and hit the ball out of the ballpark in the 1932 World Series. I wish I could have seen that. But I did see something I admired just about as much, with Satchel Paige and Babe Ruth. This was in Chicago, after Ruth came out of the major leagues. He was barnstorming, playing with different teams, and he played us. Satchel was pitching and Ruth was hitting. Satchel threw Ruth the ball and Ruth hit the ball, must have been 500 feet, off of Satchel. Satchel looked at Ruth all the way around the bases and when Ruth got to home plate, you know who shook his hand? Satchel Paige shook Ruth's hand at home plate.

"They stopped the game and waited, he and Satchel talking, until the kid went out, got the ball, brought it back and Satchel had Babe Ruth autograph that ball for him. That was some kind of moment."[61]

Ray Negron is a film producer, author and sports executive. When he was a boy someone caught him creating graffiti on a wall of Yankee Stadium. That someone happened to be George Steinbrenner, the owner of the Yankees. Steinbrenner took him under his wing and gave him a job as the Yankee bat boy which introduced Negron to the world of Billy Martin, Reggie Jackson, Thurman Munson, and other Yankees of that era. In 1975, when he was in high school, Negron was a second-round draft pick of the Pittsburgh Pirates. Today he is well known as an organizer and humanitarian, especially in the Latino community.

One of his books is a children's novel featuring the likenesses of Babe Ruth and Jackie Robinson on the cover. Though it is a work of fiction, Negron says the story is based on fact. Ruth was in attendance at Jackie Robinson's first game in the majors in 1947, and while there is no record of the two actually meeting, Negron claims that they did and fashioned a fictional tale out of it. Negron, who admits he is a 'Babe Ruth fanatic,' likes to tell the story about legendary entertainer Cab Calloway whom he had met on the set of the 1983 film *The Cotton Club*.

"We became friends and years later I ran into him at the Belmont Park racetrack," says Negron. "He was an older man and he told me about the time when he spent a whole day and night partying with Al Jolson and Babe Ruth in Harlem."

For the record, Al Jolson, like Ruth, spent time at St. Mary's Industrial School in Baltimore when he was a boy, but Ruth was there much longer than Jolson.

When people think of Babe Ruth they tend to think of home runs. It is the first thing that comes to mind and the baseball world has no shortage of descriptions about what a Babe Ruth home run was like.

Ruth biographer Robert W. Creamer may have said it best when he did an interview with Baseball Past and Present, a sports blog site, in 2012. He was eighty-nine at the time and it was only a few months before he passed away. Said Creamer: "I saw Babe play at least one game in 1932, 1933 and 1934, his last three seasons with the Yankees, and each time I saw him he hit a home run ... a couple of times it was a doubleheader and he hit a homer in one of the games ... but he hit one. In short I have the thrill of remembering what a Ruthian homer looked like up close. Simply gorgeous. That beautiful swing and Ruth's big face looking up watching it go as he starts to run. And the ball, already enormously high in the air as it floated past the infield. I mean, I saw Babe Ruth hit home runs."[62]

Those home runs turned the game around and it happened quickly. The coming of Ruth the hitter meant the end of the so-called Dead-Ball Era and the arrival of the Live-Ball Era. In 1918 Ruth, still with the Boston Red Sox, was twenty-three years old and undergoing the transition from a pitcher to an everyday outfielder. That season Ruth the pitcher started nineteen games and sported a 13-7 record with an ERA of 2.22. Ruth the hitter appeared in ninety-five games and batted an even .300. Though he wasn't yet a full-time outfielder, he still led the league in home runs with eleven.

It was a new single-season record.

The next season, 1919, was his last with the Red Sox. Ruth the pitcher started fifteen games and went 9-5 with an ERA of 2.97. Ruth the hitter played 130 games in the outfield. He hit .322 and slugged twenty-nine home runs.

In 1920 he was with the Yankees, now as a full-time outfielder. He hit .376 and wound up with the then unbelievable tally of fifty-four home runs.

In 1921 he hit .378 and got fifty-nine home runs.

Between 1918 and 1921 the total number of runs scored in Major League Baseball jumped from 7,382 to 11,928, an increase of more than 60%. And in that same time frame the total number of home runs went from 235 to 937 — an increase of almost 400%!

Brent Stevens — and his website www.BabeRuthCentral.com — keeps track of such things because he, too, is interested in preserving the legacy of his great-grandfather.

In no other sport has a single athlete had such enormous impact in so little time and the result — especially in the wake of the Black Sox scandal — was a phenomenon of unprecedented proportions. The fans came out in droves. While the 1920 New York Yankees set a new attendance record with Ruth in their lineup, teams in six other cities broke their own attendance records as well. At the time there were only sixteen teams in the big leagues. But once again, with Babe Ruth it is about more than baseball.

There are sources everywhere who cite the fact that, along with all his home runs, Babe Ruth struck out 1,330 times. They use this for inspirational and motivational purposes — from a Wall Street executive who had that strikeout total framed on the wall behind his desk to countless references in books to leadership courses in colleges throughout the land. And Ruth did strike out 1,330 times, which is almost twice the number of his 714 home runs.

Never let the fear of striking out get in the way.

On May 4, 2014, the long-time pastor of the First Presbyterian Church in Titusville, Pennsylvania gave a sermon. Dr. Barry Cressman had been the pastor for forty-two years and was soon going to retire. His sermon that day was about learning from failure and it was captured on video. It began like this:

"With the coming of spring our thoughts turn to the great American sport of baseball. For those of us of a certain vintage we invariably think of Babe Ruth as the great Sultan of Swat. But did you know that Babe Ruth struck out thirteen hundred and thirty times? And I find that a significant statistic. You and I also fail."[63]

Every strike brings me closer to the next home run.

Indeed, here was a man who came from nothing and made something of himself, and in that journey he taught valuable lessons. He had precious little education, both in school and in the greater realm of life, and yet, he is quoted and revered by world leaders, religious scholars and leading thinkers alike to this very day.

On October 26, 1935, Ruth wrote a letter to the son of his agent, Christy Walsh. It was addressed to Master Christy Walsh, Jr., St. John's Military Academy, Los Angeles, California.

Dear Christy:

Your Daddy has just told me that you are now a student at St. John's Military Academy.

When I was a young boy I attended St. Marys School in Baltimore, where the good Brothers were very patient with me and helped me a lot toward future life. I am sure the Sisters at St. John's will help you.

But the main thing in life to remember is that your success and happiness in the future will depend upon your own efforts and not the money or clothes which you might receive from your parents. The most successful men that I know today were poor boys.

Wishing you success and happiness, I am,

Yours,

Babe Ruth

That letter sold at auction in 2012 for $41,825.

In 2010 baseball writer and historian Bill Jenkinson was called upon to speak on the occasion of Babe Ruth's induction to the World Sports Humanitarian Hall of Fame. The institution had been founded

Alex Rodriguez of the New York Yankees received the Babe Ruth Home
Run Award as Major League Baseball's home run champion for 2007. He is
shown with Julia Ruth Stevens and Julia's granddaughter Amanda Dandro
at the presentation in 2008 at Yankee Stadium. There is also a Babe Ruth
Award given to the player with the best performance in the postseason.

in 1994 and is located on the campus of Boise State University in
Boise, Idaho. In his address Jenkinson spoke about "at least forty-two
different charities and organizations" Ruth was involved with, not to
mention his countless visits to hospitals, orphanages, prisons, schools,
sanitariums, what have you. He said Ruth was the first prominent
American athlete to regularly participate in philanthropic activities.
He talked about Ruth, who was of German descent, speaking out
against Nazi Germany before it became fashionable, selling War bonds
throughout World War II, and when he was gravely ill volunteering
to receive experimental treatment which may have put his life at risk
for an earlier death.

Jenkinson also spoke about race.

"As early as 1918, at age twenty-three, Ruth began his long journey to integrate Major League Baseball," he said. "Men of color from Ruth's day were well aware of Babe's efforts on their behalf, and, to a man, told me in numerous interviews of their heartfelt appreciation. In fact, the historical evidence strongly suggests that Babe Ruth did not achieve his lifelong dream of managing a Big League team because of his advocacy of integration."

Jenkinson admits there is no smoking gun, no paper or document that may have been signed by former baseball Commissioner Kenesaw Mountain Landis, or anyone else for that matter, directing the owners of Major League Baseball not to hire Ruth because of this reason. No one at Cooperstown or at the Society of American Baseball Research can provide any evidence that it was so. But Jenkinson believes this was the case and he didn't come to such a conclusion lightly.

He recalls his father taking him to a Philadelphia Athletics game in 1953 when he was six years old and how his father told him that he had seen Jimmy Foxx and Babe Ruth play.

"My Dad was a Philly fan who lived a mile from the ballpark and this was the peak of the Athletics-Yankees dynasties and it would have been natural for him to dislike Babe Ruth," Jenkinson says. "But he had countless stories about how wonderful Ruth was to all the Philadelphia kids. During the game between innings he would leave the field and go into the stands and order hot dogs and drinks for all the kids in that section. And my Dad was one of those kids. I mean who does that?"

Jenkinson recalls his aunt, his father's older sister, telling him that Ruth was always surrounded by dozens of kids and how he was like a 20th-century Pied Piper.

Before getting immersed in writing baseball books, Jenkinson made his living as a legal investigator where he said his job was "to separate fact from fiction." In the early 1980s he started exploring all the data about Ruth and his hitting prowess, and everything he found pointed in the same direction — Ruth hit the ball harder and farther than anyone who had ever played the game. It resulted in such books as 'The Year Babe Ruth Hit 104 Home Runs' (De Capo Press, 2007) and 'Baseball's Ultimate Power: Ranking The All-time Greatest Distance Home Run Hitters' (Lyons Press, 2010). Those books were the culmination of almost thirty years of research. Jenkinson meticulously went into original newspaper accounts about Ruth and his batting power. He also examined the 800 exhibition games Ruth played in his career, and did an analysis of such things as the equipment and medical sophistication during Ruth's time, and then compared that to more modern eras.

Says Jenkinson: "Did you know he tore up his knee early in his career and it always bothered him? It would have been easily repaired with modern medicine but not then."

Jenkinson made that point about Ruth's knee when he was interviewed for the TV movie Finding Babe Ruth which was made by Fox Sports Originals in 2015. In the interview he said Ruth tore the cartilage in his knee in 1918, two years before he came to the Yankees, and it didn't get surgically corrected until he was long retired at the age of forty-four. That means Ruth played on a bad knee for seventeen seasons, including his entire career with the Yankees!

In the same film sports agent Scott Boras, who has been called the top sports agent in the world, was asked how much Babe Ruth would command in the current marketplace as a free agent if he were alive in the present day. Boras said a contract worth up to *$1.5 billion* over a ten-year span wouldn't be out of the question.

"He is not a franchise player," said Boras. "He is in effect the creator of the franchise and a brand."

Jenkinson believes that 1921 was Ruth's best season when he hit fifty-nine home runs. He said that, after all his extensive analysis of the data, Ruth would have hit more than 100 home runs that year if he had been playing in modern ballparks under current rules. But this is all projection, along with his contention about Ruth not getting a managerial job because of his progressive views on race. Still, Jenkinson sticks to his guns.

He has a thick collection of old newspaper clippings with numerous mentions about Ruth becoming a manager for one team or another. The list of teams said to be interested in him as a manager included the American League's New York Yankees, Detroit Tigers and Cleveland Indians, and from the National League the Cincinnati Reds and Boston Braves. The earliest clipping is from *The Binghampton Press* and the date is October 20, 1920. Ruth had just finished his first season with the Yankees. The article, all of four paragraphs, carried the headline 'Ruth Given Chance to Manage Yankees' and in it Ruth says he was offered the job of being the Yankees' manager for the next season, but turned it down.

How does Jenkinson the baseball historian and crack investigator explain that?

"The two colonels who owned the Yankees [Col. Jacob Ruppert and Captain Tillinghast L'Hommedieu Huston] did not agree about hiring Miller Huggins as the Yankees manager," he says. "In fact, Huston was angry about that. Then they got Ruth in 1920 and even with him in the lineup they only finished third. Huston was more of a maverick owner while Ruppert was very much pro-Landis [MLB Commissioner Kenesaw Mountain Landis] but Huston was always in Ruth's corner. My guess is Huston approached him about being the team's manager but Ruth didn't want to manage at that time. He just wanted to play."

Most of the articles Jenkinson has about the possibility of Ruth becoming a manager are from 1933 and 1934. This was late in Ruth's career and at a time when he had made it known that he wanted to be a manager once his playing days are over. And that day was coming.

"Superstars becoming managers was the standard of the day," says Jenkinson, "and to a person Babe Ruth was considered a baseball genius. A brilliant tactician. But the call never came so I started looking into it. I kept bumping into all the near misses about Ruth getting a managerial job. There are just so many contradictions."

Jenkinson has an article that refers to Jacob Ruppert saying Babe Ruth would make a great manager (the term 'pilot' was used for manager in those days) and that if the job came up with another team, he (Ruppert) wouldn't stand in his way. The article in *The Washington Post* was published December 11, 1934 when the American League all-stars were not yet back from their big tour to Japan. It said:

'Ruth, touring the Orient with a barnstorming team, said he would like a managerial job, and his owner, Col. Jacob Ruppert, repeated tonight that he would release the Babe, without payment, to any club that would make him pilot. Ruppert emphasized, however, that he would not permit him to become a regular player with any other club.'

An earlier article from *The Hartford Courant*, published more than a year before that one — on October 19, 1933 — quotes Ruppert citing Ruth's managerial abilities. That article said:

"I think Ruth will make a splendid manager," Ruppert said. "He's settled down and is very serious about his future. He's talked about managing a team. I'd like to keep Ruth with the Yankees but I'll not interfere if he gets a chance to better himself."

Strangely enough, only two months later — on December 29, 1933 — the *New York Times* published a two-paragraph piece about the Cincinnati Reds trying to get Ruth as their manager and Ruppert blocking it. The story said:

'The Reds, in their quest for a new manager, tried to get Babe Ruth, but all they got was an emphatic "No!" from Colonel Jacob Ruppert of the Yankees, Larry MacPhail, general manager, disclosed today.'

"It makes no sense," says Jenkinson.

In 1933 Ruth was also said to be on the radar to manage the Detroit Tigers.

"That season the Tigers took a poll of their fans and asked them who they would like to see manage the team and they said they wanted Babe Ruth," says Jenkinson. "Frank Navin, owner of the Tigers, wanted to hire Ruth as their manager for the 1934 season. Then Ruth went to Hawaii to play some exhibition games and when he got back Navin was suddenly rethinking all this. It didn't make sense to me."

Jenkinson also has clippings about Col. Huston wanting to buy the Brooklyn Dodgers and having Ruth manage that team. And more articles still about Ruth becoming manager of the National League's Boston Braves before he left the Yankees to join the Braves, the team he would join for the 1935 season.

"I have a very thick file about the 1934 tour to Japan where Ruth was the field manager of the American League all-stars," says Jenkinson. "Connie Mack, who was the most respected manager and executive in baseball, said how Ruth managed that team under exceedingly difficult circumstances. When they got back from that tour Mack was glowing with praise about how Ruth handled the team. So what do we know?

"Babe Ruth was very pro African-American and highly regarded in the African-American community. When I first met with Julia I asked her this question. I said if Babe was a manager would he have signed black ballplayers and she said 'of course.' And she told me how disillusioned he was for the last thirteen years of his life over this business about not getting the call. In December 1934 all the owners met at the Commodore Hotel in Manhattan and Babe Ruth's future was the no. 1 issue. There was massive coverage about this nation-wide."

According to Jenkinson, while there were a few naysayers amongst the owners about Ruth becoming a manager, most of them felt he would make an excellent manager.

"I spoke to Hall of Famer Burleigh Grimes not long before he died," says Jenkinson. "He was the manager of the Brooklyn Dodgers in 1938 when they brought Ruth back from retirement to be a coach. He told me Ruth had a great baseball mind and was very smart. You know how smart he was? Dolph Camilli was a very good player who played for the Dodgers but he could never hit at Ebbets Field [home of the Dodgers] on Sundays. Ruth figured it out. Every Sunday the low center-field bleachers were full and because of all the fans sitting there and all the colors they were wearing it was hard for the batter to see the ball clearly from the batter's box. So Ruth had them erect a green screen over that section and Camilli started hitting again."

Jenkinson believes the call never went out for Ruth to be hired because he was no advocate of segregation. And Ruth never did become a manager, a sorry point that he would take with him to his grave.

"Immediately upon the death of Landis in 1944 the process of integration began when Branch Rickey started to take action," says Jenkinson. "In my mind there is no mystery here."

Jenkinson says he has spent more time and effort investigating this than anyone else. But even back in 1948 there were voices wondering how come Ruth never got to be a manager. On August 18, 1948 — two days after Babe's death — Murray Schumach wrote in the *New York Times* about how Ruth had felt let down by baseball:

> 'There was scarcely room for real bitterness in the expansive and warm Ruthian temperament, but the big fellow undoubtedly did feel at times a resentment against the owners in major league base-ball because no place in it ever was found for him. And whatever slight flame of resentment may have lighted in him was frequently fanned by many writers who openly chided the baseball moguls for sidestepping the great Bambino.'

In 2008 Bill Jenkinson spoke at an event honoring the sixtieth anniversary of Ruth's death and it was at the very same St. Patrick's Cathedral in New York where Ruth's funeral had been held in 1948. It was effectively a eulogy and Jenkinson explains that no eulogy for Ruth had ever taken place at the actual funeral mass because, he says, Cardinal Spellman did not consider his own remarks to be a eulogy. Some 2,500 people turned out for the sixtieth anniversary.

On that Saturday afternoon at St. Patrick's Cathedral — it was held September 6, 2008 — Jenkinson talked about the profound grief that engulfed the nation when Ruth died. And why was that?

"I think it was about hope," he said in his remarks.

He then related the story of Ruth's life and times. How he had been born into relative poverty. That he had spent twelve years in a reform school and had been poorly educated. How he had battled a weight problem for most of his career. And the countless injuries he had suffered because of his aggressive style of play.

"Life had a way of regularly knocking Babe Ruth down," Jenkinson said that afternoon. "But he always got back up, and when he did he swung for the fences. And Americans everywhere loved him for it.

"He imbued them with hope. They saw this unlikely man constantly overcoming adversity despite his humble origins, and they applied his inspiration to the problems in their own lives. Tired men would think, if Babe Ruth could overcome his most recent problem, they could get up the next morning and go to work. Quarrelling neighbors would look at Ruth's life and say that they could somehow find a way to get along. Despondent daughters would hear the story of Babe Ruth's life and summon the energy to care for their sick mothers. Whenever people thought about the Babe their spirits brightened and their steps became a little lighter. Despite his fame and fortune everyone related to him. Regardless of their situation in life, everybody felt a kinship to Babe Ruth. They were one with him.

"So as we meet in this sacred and majestic house of worship to honor this unique man, we should honor him for the right reasons. We should recognize his greatest contribution to our common American heritage. It wasn't the baseball records that he left us. It was his legacy of hope."

Babe Ruth is buried at Gate of Heaven Cemetery in Hawthorne, New York, in Westchester County. It is twenty-five miles north of New York City. Gate of Heaven is one of the most famous cemeteries in America and boasts scores of recognizable names and celebrities from all walks of life. The list includes actors James Cagney and Sal Mineo, journalist Dorothy Kilgallen, mobster Dutch Schultz, Bess Houdini who was the wife of magician Harry Houdini, former New York City Mayor Jimmy Walker, not to mention such baseball luminaries as Billy Martin and pitcher Ralph Branca who is best remembered for giving up a Bobby Thomson home run that came to be known as the Shot Heard 'Round the World. That was in a 1951 playoff game.

But Babe Ruth is the biggest name of all.

On February 6, 2014, an article by sportswriter Spencer Fordin was posted on MLB.com. It was called 'Ruth's gravesite remains a phenomenon.' The article included an interview with a man named Andrew Nagle, who worked for the Archdiocese of New York which operated the cemetery. Said Nagle:

> "I'm in this business for forty years. I've worked non-sectarian cemeteries and I've worked in a famous cemetery in the Bronx called Woodlawn. There are a lot of famous people buried at Woodlawn — F.W. Woolworth, J.C. Penney, Rowland Macy, Isidor Straus who went down with the Titanic, Herman Melville, the guy who wrote 'Moby Dick.' But no graves are visited like Babe Ruth's grave."[64]

Ruth's second wife Claire is buried next to him and engraved on the monument is an image of Jesus with his arm around a boy who looks to be a ballplayer. To the right Ruth's name is carved in stone. *George Herman Ruth*. And the years *1895-1948*. And below that the name *Claire Ruth*. And the years *1900-1976*. To the left is an inscription attributed to Cardinal Spellman who had officiated at the funeral.

"May the divine spirit that animated Babe Ruth to win the crucial game of life inspire the youth of America."

Sometimes, tour buses come. Always there are things left behind by the trail of countless visitors. People have left hot dogs in buns. Once a pizza was delivered and just placed there on the grave. On any given day one may find flowers, lucky pennies, baseball gloves, baseball cards, bats, Baby Ruth candy bars, balloons, pennants, cigars,

American flags, you name it. Usually there are baseballs. A recent visit saw a pair of miniature New York Yankee batting helmets on either side of the monument and folded in between them was a handwritten note that said 'Babe, make me a better ball player.'

It was signed *Audrey.*

Lou Gehrig is buried not more than a mile away at Kensico Cemetery.

There are statues, monuments and plaques for Babe Ruth all over the United States and around the world. At Camden Yards in Baltimore the towering, sixteen-foot bronze statue of a young Ruth called *Babe's Dream* was unveiled at an Orioles' game with its creator, Susan Luery, and Babe's daughter Julia Ruth Stevens, on hand. On that day they had performed the duty of throwing out the game ball.

There is another statue of him at the Sports Immortals Museum in Boca Raton, Florida. Inscribed on the plinth base holding the statue it says:

BABE RUTH. 1895-1948. A MAN NEVER STANDS SO TALL AS WHEN HE STOOPS TO HELP A CHILD.

Those statues were erected in 1995 and 1996, 1995 being the centennial of Ruth's birth.

In Fayetteville, North Carolina there is a historical marker commemorating his first home run as a professional, that one in a pre-season, intra-squad game on March 7, 1914. The marker reads:

BABE RUTH. Hit his first home run in professional baseball, March, 1914. 135 yds. N.W. In this town George Herman Ruth acquired the nickname "Babe."

Jack Dunn was the owner and manager of the International League Baltimore Orioles — a minor-league team — and the young rookie Ruth was dubbed 'Dunn's baby,' hence the name Babe. The home run in Fayetteville was hit by Ruth, a pitcher, in his first ever game as a pro. It was his second time at bat.

Not to be outdone, the city of Toronto in Canada also claims his first home run, that occurring in an official league game in the minors on September 5, 1914. The plaque was unveiled in 2006 in a ceremony involving representatives from the New York Yankees and Toronto Blue Jays with Ruth's grandson Tom Stevens the guest of honor.

Tampa, Florida has a plaque celebrating *BABE'S LONGEST HOMER*. That would be his 587-foot home run in a pre-season game played at Tampa's Plant Field on April 4, 1919. Ruth was with the Red Sox then and they were playing against the New York Giants.

In Wilkes-Barre, Pennsylvania there is a sign celebrating *The Longest Home Run in Competitive Baseball History*. They say Ruth hit that one 650 feet in a barnstorming game in 1926 and, for the record, there are also other towns that make the claim about the longest home run ever hit by Babe Ruth.

Hot Springs, Arkansas has a different take on it by claiming the first ever 500-foot home run. The plaque there reads:

> *BABE RUTH. Ruth trained here nine times and became a very familiar face around Hot Springs. He hiked the mountains, took the baths, played golf, patronized the casinos, and visited the racetrack. On March 17, 1918 (St. Patrick's Day), he launched a mammoth home run from Whittington Park that landed on the fly inside the Arkansas Alligator Farm. It has been measured at 573 feet, baseball's first 500-foot-plus drive.*

That plaque went up in 2012.

In Japan there is the plaque at Koshien Stadium in Osaka and the statue at Yagiyama Zoological Park in Sendai City, and, of course, there is the life-size basswood sculpture of Ruth at the National Baseball Hall of Fame in Cooperstown.

Today at Yankee Stadium, the new Yankee Stadium that opened the 2009 season, Babe Ruth Plaza can be found between Gates 4 and 6 on the south side of the stadium. And then there is the monument.

The original granite monument for Ruth was one of six installed over the years at Monument Park. The first was for Yankees manager Miller Huggins and then came Gehrig and Ruth. After Ruth it was Joe DiMaggio and Mickey Mantle, and then a final one for the victims of September 11, 2001. In 2008 all those monuments were moved to the new Yankee Stadium.

On Ruth's monument, just below the face that everyone knows, are his name *BABE RUTH* and the years of his all-too-short life. *1895-1948*. At the bottom it says *Erected by the Yankees and the New York Baseball Writers, April 19, 1949* and in the middle are ten words.

A great ballplayer, a great man, and a great American.

And he was. He was all those things. But they could have added something else that is just as true.

One of a kind.

Julia was right. There will never be another like him.

Acknowledgments

I DON'T REMEMBER when I first got the idea to write this book. But for sure it was one of those 'Aha!' moments which often get portrayed with the image of a light bulb going on. My novel *Gift of the Bambino*, a work of fiction, required extensive research on Babe Ruth and the more I learned the more fascinating a character he became for me.

Over the years I did a number of articles about him and kept coming across elements of the enormous legacy that he left. This includes Babe Ruth League baseball, which is thriving today and bigger than ever, and the Babe Ruth Birthplace and Museum in Baltimore. It also includes his huge presence at the National Baseball Hall of Fame and Museum in Cooperstown, the whole business of sports memorabilia and Ruth's undisputed role as the no. 1 player in the industry, the commercial appeal and endorsement power of the name Babe Ruth, not to mention the huge impact he has had in Japan and many other countries around the world.

Tom Stevens is the Babe's grandson and son of Julia Ruth Stevens, who is the Babe's daughter. We first met in 2006 at an event commemorating the 1914 home run at Hanlan's Point in Toronto, the site of Ruth's first pro home run in an official league game when he was a minor leaguer. Tom was the guest of honor and threw out the game ball that evening in a match between the New York Yankees and Toronto Blue Jays. He later read my novel and liked it. Since then we have stayed in touch. At some point I mentioned to him this idea about doing a book on the legacy of the Babe. Despite all the books written about Babe Ruth over the years, no one has ever done such a book before.

Tom was on board immediately and that culminated in a remarkable afternoon for me with Julia at the family home in New Hampshire.

Tom and his son Brent Stevens are both dedicated to preserving the legacy of the Babe, and I can't thank them enough for all their help with this book. Of course, the same holds true for Julia.

I have also been involved in research and countless interviews with other key people who keep the Ruth legacy alive. And I want to thank them all.

Steve Tellefsen, who leads Babe Ruth League baseball, has been most helpful and gracious in telling me everything there is to know about this remarkable organization and how it got to be what it is. He and his father have been the only presidents of BRL since 1980.

I am indebted to long-time Ruth aficionado Michael Gibbons, who has spent the better part of four decades running the Babe Ruth Birthplace and Museum in Baltimore. His staff and especially Shawn Herne must also be thanked.

Tom Shieber, senior curator at the Baseball Hall of Fame and Museum in Cooperstown, gave me a personal tour of the revised Babe Ruth exhibit. Also, from the Hall of Fame I want to thank Jeff Idelson, Jim Gates, John Thorn, and Cassidy Lent who not only answered my many questions but lugged out each and every volume of the twenty-five Babe Ruth scrapbooks during my visit to the Giamatti Research Center at the Hall of Fame's incredible library.

James Barber, Curator of the National Portrait Gallery at the Smithsonian in Washington, D.C., was also very helpful in helping me understand what went into Babe Ruth's One Life exhibit that wound up in June, 2017. Also a big 'thank you' goes out to Erin Beasley at the Smithsonian.

Pete Enfield of The Luminary Group was the recipient of countless phone calls and emails from me as I tried to learn all about the business of the merchandising of the Babe Ruth name, and he answered every question I threw at him and provided an insight into this fascinating industry. Special thanks must also go to Benjamin Kaufman and Thomas Ramdahl of Norwegian Airlines, and Ben Ecklar of Panini America.

From the world of sports memorabilia and collecting I am indebted to a number of people. They include David Kohler of SCP Auctions, Mike Heffner of Lelands, Joe Orlando and Kevin Keating of PSA, Ray Schulte, and Scott Ireland. Thanks also to Chris Meiman of the Louisville Slugger Museum & Factory.

In addition, there were several authors and researchers who have written books about and involving Babe Ruth. Each and every one of them was most generous and helpful. The list includes Robert K. Fitts, Robert Whiting, Will Michaels, Tim Reid, Dennis Corcoran, the late Robert Creamer, and of course, baseball historian and researcher Bill Jenkinson who was most patient with my relentless pursuit of information. I also must include sculptor Susan Luery.

Special thanks also goes to Ryozo Kato, the former Japanese ambassador to the United States and former Commissioner of Nippon Professional Baseball, his wife Hanayo Kato, as well as Kazuo Sayama, Manuel Marquez-Sterling, Tchavdar Georgiev, Marty Appel, Ray Negron, and Sean Gibson. In Canada I want to thank Barry Naymark, Bill Humber, Andrew North, Tom Valcke, and my incredible designer Tania Craan.

Finally, I must thank Babe Ruth himself for just being the Babe.

Julia was a guest of the Boston Red Sox
when she was 100 years old.

Notes

Chapter 1

1   April 4, 2015, Brian Gray, CEO, Leaf Trading Cards,
http://www.baberuthcentral.com/leaf-trading-cards-strikes-deal-babe/

2   http://hofmag.blogspot.ca/2006/08/why-babe-ruth-still-matters.html

Chapter 2

3   https://www.prnewswire.com/news-releases/millennials-and-baby-boomer-baseball-fans-agree--babe-ruth-is-the-goat-300484807.html

4   http://northeastjournal.org/wp-content/uploads/2017/03/NEJ-MarApr2017.pdf

5   *The Babe and I* by Claire Merritt Hodgson and Bill Slocum (Prentice-Hall, 1959)

6   *The Babe and I* by Claire Merritt Hodgson and Bill Slocum (Prentice-Hall, 1959)

7   *The Babe and I* by Claire Merritt Hodgson and Bill Slocum (Prentice-Hall, 1959)

8   *Lefty — An American Odyssey* by Vernona Gomez and Lawrence Goldstone (Ballantine Books, New York 2012)

9   https://www.forbes.com/2009/03/23/baseball-cards-expensive-lifestyle-collecting-baseball-cards.html

Chapter 3

10   http://www.nytimes.com/learning/general/onthisday/bday/0206.html

11   http://www.baberuthcentral.com/babesimpact/memborabilia-collection/western-union-telegrams/

12   Ibid

13   Ibid

14   Ibid

15   Ibid

16   Ibid

17   http://www.nytimes.com/2004/11/29/obituaries/murray-schumach-neighborhood-storyteller-dies-at-91.html

18   *The New York Times*, August 18, 1948

19   Ibid

20   Ibid

21   *The Babe Book* by Ernestine Miller (Andrews McMeel Publishing, Kansas City 2000)

22   *The Babe Book* by Ernestine Miller (Andrews McMeel Publishing, Kansas City 2000)

23   https://entertainment.howstuffworks.com/babe-ruth44.htm

24   *The Babe Book* by Ernestine Miller (Andrews McMeel Publishing, Kansas City 2000)

Chapter 4

25   http://www.npr.org/2011/03/16/134570236/the-secret-history-of-baseballs-earliest-days

26   Induction Day at Cooperstown by Dennis Corcoran (McFarland & Company, Inc. 2011)

27   Induction Day at Cooperstown by Dennis Corcoran (McFarland & Company, Inc. 2011)

28   Ibid

29   *The Babe and I* by Claire Merritt Hodgson and Bill Slocum (Prentice-Hall, 1959)

Chapter 6

30   https://www.baberuthleague.org/media/11373/Jordan.pdf

Chapter 7

31 http://www.script-o-rama.com/movie_scripts/s/sandlot-script-transcript-baseball-leary.html

Chapter 8

32 http://www.chron.com/business/article/Moneymakers-Jeffrey-Rosenberg-1558366.php
33 https://www.forbes.com/sites/kurtbadenhausen/2017/07/12/the-cowboys-and-yankees-top-the-worlds-most-valuable-sports-teams-of-2017/#63ec8cb65018
34 http://www.stockpickssystem.com/historical-rate-of-return
35 https://www.psacard.com/lists/top-20-baseball-autographs
36 (https://financesonline.com/10-of-the-worlds-most-expensive-autographs-whose-signatures-are-now-worth-a-fortune/
37 www.thesportster.com/entertainment/top-15-most-expensive-pieces-of-sports-memorabilia-ever-sold/
38 https://www.justcollecting.com/miscellania/sports-memorabilia-collecting-a-history

Chapter 9

39 *The Babe Book* by Ernestine Miller (Andrews McMeel Publishing, Kansas City 2000)

Chapter 10

40 *Banzai Babe Ruth* by Robert K. Fitts (University of Nebraska Press, Lincoln and London 2012), pg 120
41 *The Babe Ruth Story by Babe Ruth and Bob Considine*, (E. P. Dutton & Company, 1948)
42 *Banzai Babe Ruth* by Robert K. Fitts, (University of Nebraska Press, Lincoln and London, 2012)
43 *Banzai Babe Ruth* by Robert K. Fitts, (University of Nebraska Press, Lincoln and London, 2012)
44 *Miracle Man of Japan* by Edward Uhlan and Dana L. Thomas (Exposition Press, New York, 1957)
45 *Miracle Man of Japan* by Edward Uhlan and Dana L. Thomas (Exposition Press, New York, 1957)
46 *Banzai Babe Ruth* by Robert K. Fitts, (University of Nebraska Press, Lincoln and London, 2012)
47 *The Babe Ruth Story by Babe Ruth and Bob Considine*, (E. P. Dutton & Company, 1948)
48 *Babe — The Legend Comes to Life* by Robert W. Creamer (Simon & Schuster, New York 1974
49 *The Toronto Star*, September 5, 2003
50 http://asiafoundation.org/2017/09/06/baseball-diplomacy/

Chapter 11

51 *The Babe Ruth Story by Babe Ruth as told to Bob Considine*,(E. P. Dutton & Company, 1948)
52 Ibid
53 Ibid
54 Ibid
55 Ibid
56 http://www.nytimes.com/1973/09/16/archives/one-of-a-kind-the-babe-was-always-a-boy.html
57 https://www.espn.com/sportscentury/features/00242487.html
58 http://www.baberuth.com/quotes/
59 Ibid
60 https://sabr.org/bioproj/person/df02083c
61 http://www.pbs.org/kenburns/baseball/shadowball/oneil.html
62 http://baseballpastandpresent.com/2012/01/17/interview-robert-creamer/
63 https://www.youtube.com/watch?v=Ie4MIubUx5Y
64 http://m.mlb.com/news/article/67494458/babe-ruths-gravesite-remains-destination-for-faithful-fans/

Photo Credits

Cover

Page 3 — Scott Ireland and SCP Auctions

Foreword

Page 15 — Babe Ruth Central

Chapter 1

Page 23 — View of "One Life: Babe Ruth." Photo by Matailong Du/National Portrait Gallery, Smithsonian Institution
Page 28 — View of "One Life: Babe Ruth." Photo by Matailong Du/National Portrait Gallery, Smithsonian Institution
Page 29 — View of "One Life: Babe Ruth." Photo by Matailong Du/National Portrait Gallery, Smithsonian Institution
Page 33 — View of "One Life: Babe Ruth." Photo by Matailong Du/National Portrait Gallery, Smithsonian Institution

Chapter 2

Page 37 — Babe Ruth Central
Page 43 — Babe Ruth Central
Page 47 — Babe Ruth Central
Page 48 — Babe Ruth Central
Page 55 — Babe Ruth Central
Page 60 — Jerry Amernic

Chapter 3

Page 63 — Used with permission by Louisville Slugger Museum & Factory®
Page 74 — Babe Ruth Central

Chapter 4

Page 77 — National Baseball Hall of Fame and Museum
Page 84 — National Baseball Hall of Fame and Museum
Page 85 (top) — National Baseball Hall of Fame and Museum
Page 85 (bottom) — National Baseball Hall of Fame and Museum
Page 87 — National Baseball Hall of Fame and Museum
Page 89 — National Baseball Hall of Fame and Museum

Chapter 5

Page 97 — Babe Ruth Birthplace & Museum
Page 101 — Babe Ruth Birthplace & Museum
Page 102 — Babe Ruth Birthplace & Museum
Page 105 — Babe Ruth Birthplace & Museum
Page 106 — Babe Ruth Birthplace & Museum

Index

About the Author

JERRY AMERNIC is a writer of fiction and non-fiction books who lives in Toronto. He has been a newspaper reporter and correspondent, newspaper columnist, feature writer for magazines, and media consultant. He is a graduate of the University of Toronto.

His first book was *VICTIMS: The Orphans of Justice*, the true story of a man who galvanized victims of violent crime after his own daughter was murdered. More recently, Jerry worked with Julian Fantino, former Chief of the Toronto Police Service and former Commissioner of the Ontario Provincial Police, on Mr. Fantino's memoir *DUTY — The Life of a Cop*. For several years Jerry wrote a column about the criminal justice system called Justice For All in Toronto's Sunday Sun newspaper.

On the fiction front Jerry's debut novel was *Gift of the Bambino* which received rave reviews in both Canada and the United States. The book is about a boy and his grandfather, and how they are bound by baseball and the spirit of Babe Ruth. In 2006 Jerry was involved in a commemorative event marking Babe Ruth's first professional home run in an official league game — it was his only minor-league home run — which took place in 1914 at Hanlan's Point in Toronto. Jerry has written many articles about Babe Ruth and has done a great deal of research on him.

His other works of fiction are *The Last Witness*, his highly acclaimed novel about the last living survivor of the Holocaust in the near future, and *Qumran*, a biblical-historical page-turner about an archeologist who makes a dramatic discovery in the Holy Land.

About the Cover

This photograph of Babe Ruth at age twenty-five was taken by A. R. Smith in the Yankees' dugout during a game in 1920. Ruth had already made the transition from a pitcher to full-time outfielder. In the 1920 season, his first with the Yankees, he set a new record for home runs with fifty-four. The framed photograph was signed by Ruth the following year and was purchased in 2004 by collector Scott Ireland for $149,500 at an auction in New York City. It was the first single-signed photograph to ever break the $100,000 mark.